ESSAYS
ON THE
INTELLECT

Edited by
Frances R. Link

Association for Supervision and Curriculum Development
225 N. Washington Street
Alexandria, VA 22314
(703) 549-9110

ASCD publications present a variety of viewpoints. The views expressed or implied in this publication are not necessarily official positions of the Association.

Price: $5.00
ASCD Stock Number: 611-85408
ISBN: 0-87120-132-1
Library of Congress
  Card Catalog Number: 84-81488

Contents

Foreword

At a time of avid public interest in quality education, it is significant to note what John Goodlad discovered when he surveyed what people consider to be the goals of schooling. Whether he asked parents, teachers, or students, he found that the intellectual development of students was consistently identified as the *most* important goal of schooling. Goodlad described intellectual development as developing the ability to think rationally, including problem-solving skills, application of principles of logic, and skill in using different modes of inquiry.[1]

The Association for Supervision and Curriculum Development has been working at the forefront of a national movement aimed at helping students become more effective thinkers. While our primary efforts have been directed toward approaches to staff development and curriculum development for thinking, we have also recognized the need to provide a broader perspective on the topic of intellectual development lest we be guilty of not seeing the forest for the trees.

In designing *Essays on the Intellect*, Francis Link has invited some leading scholars and researchers to share their perspectives and findings on this important topic. Their work provides a look at the "forest" within which our work on student thinking is growing. For those of us whose daily work is concentrated on specific efforts at improving student thinking, it is an opportunity to take one step back and reflect on broader perspectives.

Carolyn Hughes
ASCD President, 1985-86

[1] John I. Goodlad, *A Place Called School* (New York: McGraw-Hill, 1984), p.39.

Introduction

An essay is an analytic or interpretive composition dealing with its subject from a limited or personal point of view. This collection of essays is intended to bring to the reader the ideas of a selected group of authors whose work relates to a range of topics and interpretations of personal research or fields related to intellectual development.

Interest in intellectual development is no new phenomenon. Psychologists, scientists, and educators have periodically come together over the last two decades to relate their findings and concerns to curriculum development. However, in the past five years there has been a marked increase in activity in theoretical and practical approaches to study of the human mind and the dynamics related to the development of the intellect.

There has been a flood of publications concerned with the teaching of thinking and problem solving, a great many exploring definitions and approaches to instruction. This book explores the implications of recent theoretical positions as in the work of Elliott Jaques, Joseph Walters, and Howard Gardner; examines the long interest and study of intellectual development with the gifted and talented, which has occupied Harry Passow's attention for more than a decade; and examines specific theoretical and related curricular approaches described in the essays by Allan Glatthorn, Robert Sternberg, Frances Link, and Garry McDaniels. Wherever possible, these authors analyze how their ideas might contribute to our thinking about educational planning. Some essays you will want to read and re-read. The sequence is your choice.

Frances R. Link,
Editor

1. The Development and Education of Intelligences

Joseph M. Walters and Howard Gardner

The Theory of Multiple Intelligences

Contrasting Points of View

Two 11-year-old children are taking a test of "intelligence." They sit at their desks laboring over the meanings of different words, the interpretation of graphs, and the solutions to arithmetic problems. They record their answers by filling in small circles on a single piece of paper. Later these completed answer sheets are scored objectively: the number of right answers is converted into a standardized score that compares the individual child with a population of children of similar age.

The teachers of these children review the different scores. They notice that one of the children has performed at a superior level; on all sections of the test, she answered more questions correctly than did her peers. In fact, her score is similar to that of children three to four years older. The other child's performance is "average"—his scores reflect those of other children his age.

Authors' note: The research reported in this chapter was supported by grants from the Bernard van Leer Foundation of The Hague, the Spencer Foundation of Chicago, and the Carnegie Corporation of New York. We are grateful to Mara Krechevsky, who gave many helpful comments on earlier drafts.

A subtle change in expectations surrounds the review of these test scores. Teachers begin to expect the first child to do quite well during her formal schooling, whereas the second should have only moderate success. Indeed these predictions come true. In other words, the test taken by the 11-year-olds serves as a reliable predictor of their later performance in school.

How does this happen? One explanation involves our free use of the word "intelligence": the child with the greater "intelligence" has the ability to solve problems, to find the answers to specific questions, and to learn new material quickly and efficiently. These skills in turn play a central role in school success. In this view, "intelligence" is a singular faculty that is brought to bear in any problem-solving situation. Since schooling deals largely with solving problems of various sorts, predicting this capacity in young children predicts their future success in school.

"Intelligence," from this point of view, is a general ability that is found in varying degrees in all individuals. It is the key to success in solving problems. This ability can be measured reliably with standardized pencil-and-paper tests that, in turn, predict future success in school.

What happens after school is completed? Consider the two individuals in the example. Looking further down the road, we find that the "average" student has become a highly successful mechanical engineer who has risen to a position of prominence in both the professional community of engineers as well as in civic groups in his community. His success is no fluke—he is considered by all to be a talented individual. The "superior" student, on the other hand, has had little success in her chosen career as a writer; after repeated rejections by publishers, she has taken up a middle management position in a bank. While certainly not a "failure," she is considered by her peers to be quite "ordinary" in her adult accomplishments. So what happened?

This fabricated example is based on the facts of intelligence testing. IQ tests predict school performance with considerable accuracy, but they are only an indifferent predictor of performance in a profession after formal schooling (Jencks, 1972). Furthermore, even as IQ tests measure only logical or logical-linguistic capacities, in this society we are nearly "brain-washed" to restrict the notion of intelligence to the capacities used in solving logical and linguistic problems.

To introduce an alternative point of view, undertake the following *Gedanken* experiment. Suspend the usual judgment of what constitutes intelligence and let your thoughts run freely over the capabilities of humans—perhaps those that would be picked out by the proverbial

Martian visitor. In this exercise, you are drawn to the brilliant chess player, the world-class violinist, and the champion athlete; such outstanding performers deserve special consideration. Under this experiment, a quite different view of *intelligence* emerges. Are the chess player, violinist, and athlete "intelligent" in these pursuits? If they are, then why do our tests of "intelligence" fail to identify them? If they are not "intelligent," what allows them to achieve such astounding feats? In general, why does the contemporary construct "intelligence" fail to explain large areas of human endeavor?

In this chapter we approach these problems through the theory of Multiple Intelligences (MI). As the name indicates, we believe that human cognitive competence is better described in terms of a set of abilities, talents, or mental skills, which we call "Intelligences." All normal individuals possess each of these skills to some extent; individuals differ in the degree of skill and in the nature of their combination. We believe this theory of intelligence may be more humane and more veridical than alternative views of intelligence and that it more adequately reflects the data of human "intelligent" behavior. Such a theory has important educational implications, including ones for curriculum development.

What Constitutes an Intelligence?

The question of the optimal definition of "intelligence" looms large in our inquiry. Indeed, it is at the level of this definition that the theory of Multiple Intelligences diverges from more traditional points of view. In a more traditional view, intelligence is defined operationally as the ability to answer items on tests of intelligence. The inference from the test scores to some underlying ability is supported by statistical techniques that compare responses of subjects at different ages; the apparent correlation of these test scores across ages and across different tests corroborates the notion that the general faculty of intelligence, "g," does not change much with age nor with training or experience. It is an inborn attribute or faculty of the individual.

Multiple Intelligences theory, on the other hand, pluralizes the traditional concept. An Intelligence entails the ability to solve problems or fashion products that are of consequence in a particular cultural setting. The problem-solving skill allows one to approach a situation in which a goal is to be obtained and to locate the appropriate route to that goal. The creation of a *cultural* product is crucial to such functions as capturing and transmitting knowledge or expressing one's views or feelings. The problems to be solved range from creating an end to a story to anticipating a mating move in chess to repairing a quilt. Products range from scientific theories to musical compositions to successful political campaigns.

MI theory is framed in light of the biological origins of each problem-solving skill. Only those skills that are universal to the human species are treated. Even so, the biological proclivity to participate in a particular form of problem solving must also be coupled with the cultural nurturing of that domain. For example, language, a universal skill, may manifest itself particularly as writing in one culture, as oratory in another culture, and as the secret language of anagrams in a third.

Given the desire of selecting Intelligences that are rooted in biology, and which are valued in one or more cultural settings, how does one actually identify an "Intelligence"? In coming up with our list, we consulted evidence from several different sources: knowledge about normal development and development in gifted individuals; information about the breakdown of cognitive skills under conditions of brain damage; studies of exceptional populations, including prodigies, idiots savants, and autistic children; data about the evolution of cognition over the millenia; cross-cultural accounts of cognition; psychometric studies, including examinations of correlations among tests; and psychological training studies, particularly measures of transfer and generalization across tasks. Only those candidate Intelligences that satisfied all or a majority of the criteria were selected as bona fide Intelligences. A more complete discussion of each of these criteria for an "Intelligence" and the seven Intelligences that have been proposed so far, is found in Gardner's book, *Frames of Mind* (1983). This book also considers how the theory might be disproven and compares it to competing theories of intelligence.

In addition to satisfying the aforementioned criteria, each Intelligence must have an identifiable core operation or set of operations. As a neurally based computational system, each Intelligence is activated or "triggered" by certain kinds of internally or externally presented information. For example, one core of Musical Intelligence is the sensitivity to pitch relations, whereas one core of Linguistic Intelligence is the sensitivity to phonological features.

An Intelligence must also be susceptible to encoding in a symbol system—a culturally contrived system of meaning, which captures and conveys important forms of information. Language, picturing, and mathematics are but three nearly worldwide symbol systems that are necessary for human survival and productivity. The relationship of a candidate Intelligence to a human symbol system is no accident. In fact, the existence of a core computational capacity anticipates the existence of a symbol system which exploits that capacity. While it may be possible for an Intelligence to proceed without an accompanying symbol system, a primary characteristic of human intelligence may well be its gravitation toward such an embodiment.

The Seven Intelligences

Having sketched the characteristics and criteria of an Intelligence, we turn now to a brief consideration of each of the seven Intelligences. We begin each sketch with a thumbnail biography of a person who demonstrates an unusual facility with that Intelligence. These biographies illustrate some of the abilities that are central to the fluent operation of a given Intelligence. Although each biography illustrates a particular Intelligence, we do not wish to imply that in adulthood Intelligences operate in isolation. Indeed, except for abnormal individuals, Intelligences always work in concert, and any sophisticated adult role will involve a melding of several of them. Following each biography we survey the various sources of data that support each candidate as an "Intelligence."

Musical Intelligence

When he was three years old, Yehudi Menuhin was smuggled into the San Francisco Orchestra concerts by his parents. The sound of Louis Persinger's violin so entranced the youngster that he insisted on a violin for his birthday and Louis Persinger as his teacher. He got both. By the time he was ten years old, Menuhin was an international performer (Menuhin, 1977).

Violinist Yehudi Menuhin's Musical Intelligence manifested itself even before he had touched a violin or received any musical training. His powerful reaction to that particular sound and his rapid progress on the instrument suggest that he was biologically prepared in some way for that endeavor. In this way evidence from child prodigies supports our claim that there is a biological link to a particular Intelligence. Other special populations, such as autistic children who can play a musical instrument beautifully but who cannot speak, underscore the independence of Musical Intelligence.

A brief consideration of the evidence suggests that musical skill passes the other tests for an Intelligence. For example, certain parts of the brain play important roles in perception and production of music. These areas are characteristically located in the right hemisphere, although musical skill is not as clearly "localized," or located in specifiable area, as language. Although the particular susceptibility of musical ability to brain damage depends on the degree of training and other individual differences, there is clear evidence for "amusia" or loss of musical ability.

Music apparently played an important unifying role in Stone Age societies. Birdsong provides a link to other species. Evidence from various cultures supports the notion that music is a universal faculty. Studies of infant development suggest that there is a "raw" computational ability in early childhood. Finally, musical notation provides an accessible and lucid symbol system.

In short, evidence to support the interpretation of musical ability as an "Intelligence" comes from many different sources. Even though musical skill is not typically considered an intellectual skill like mathematics, it qualifies under our criteria. By definition it deserves consideration; and in view of the data, its inclusion is empirically justified.

Bodily-Kinesthetic Intelligence

Fifteen-year-old Babe Ruth played third base. During one game his team's pitcher was doing very poorly and Babe loudly criticized him from third base. Brother Mathias, the coach, called out, "Ruth, if you know so much about it, YOU pitch!" Babe was surprised and embarrassed because he had never pitched before, but Brother Mathias insisted. Ruth said later that at the very moment he took the pitcher's mound, he KNEW he was supposed to be a pitcher and that it was "natural" for him to strike people out. Indeed, he went on to become a great major league pitcher (and, of course, legendary status as a hitter) (Connor, 1982).

Like Menuhin, Babe Ruth was a child prodigy who recognized his "instrument" immediately upon his first exposure to it. This recognition occurred in advance of formal training.

Control of bodily movement is, of course, localized in the motor cortex, with each hemisphere dominant or controlling bodily movements on the contra-lateral side. In right-handers, the dominance for such movement is ordinarily found in the left hemisphere. The ability to perform movements when directed to do so can be impaired even in individuals who can perform the same movements reflexively or on a nonvoluntary basis. The existence of specific *apraxia* constitutes one line of evidence for a Bodily-Kinesthetic Intelligence.

The evolution of specialized body movements is of obvious advantage to the species, and in humans this adaptation is extended through the use of tools. Body movement undergoes a clearly defined developmental schedule in children. And there is little question of its universality across cultures. Thus it appears that bodily-kinesthetic "knowledge" satisfies many of the criteria for an Intelligence.

Perhaps more difficult, however, is the consideration of bodily-kinesthetic knowledge as "problem solving." Certainly carrying out a mime sequence or hitting a tennis ball is not solving a mathematical equation. And yet, the ability to use one's body to express an emotion (as in a dance), to play a game (as in a sport) or to create a new product (as in devising an invention) are evidence of the cognitive features of body usage. The specific computations required to solve a particular bodily-kinesthetic *problem*, hitting a tennis ball, are summarized by Tim Gallwey:

At the moment the ball leaves the server's racket, the brain calculates approximately where it will land and where the racket will intercept it. This calculation includes the initial velocity of the ball, combined with an input for the progressive decrease in velocity and the effect of wind and after the bounce of the ball. Simultaneously, muscle orders are given: not just once, but constantly with refined and updated information. The muscles must cooperate. A movement of the feet occurs, the racket is taken back, the face of the racket kept at a constant angle. Contact is made at a precise point that depends on whether the order was given to hit down the line or cross-court, an order not given until after a split-second analysis of the movement and balance of the opponent.

To return an average serve, you have about one second to do this. To hit the ball at all is remarkable and yet not uncommon. The truth is that everyone who inhabits a human body possesses a remarkable creation (Gallwey, 1976).

Logical-Mathematical Intelligence

In 1983 Barbara McClintock won the *Nobel Prize in Medicine or Physiology* for her work in microbiology. Her intellectual powers of deduction and observation illustrate one form of Logical-Mathematical Intelligence that is often labeled "scientific thinking." One incident is particularly illuminating. While a researcher at Cornell in the 1920s McClintock was faced one day with a problem: while *theory* predicted 50 percent pollen sterility in corn, her research assistant (in the "field") was finding plants that were only 25 to 30 percent sterile. Disturbed by this discrepancy, McClintock left the cornfield and returned to her office where she sat for half an hour, thinking:

Suddenly I jumped up and ran back to the (corn) field. At the top of the field (the others were still at the bottom) I shouted "Eureka, I have it! I know what the 30% sterility is!" . . . They asked me to prove it. I sat down with a paper bag and a pencil and I started from scratch, which I had not done at all in my laboratory. It had all been done so fast; the answer came and I ran. Now I worked it out step by step—it was an intricate series of steps—and I came out with [the same result]. [They] looked at the material and it was exactly as I'd said it was; it worked out exactly as I had diagrammed it. Now, why did I know, without having done it on paper? Why was I so sure? (Keller, 1982, p. 104).

This anecdote illustrates two essential facts of the Logical-Mathematical Intelligence. First, in the gifted individual, the process of problem solving is often remarkably rapid—the successful scientist copes with many variables at once and creates numerous hypotheses that are each evaluated and then accepted or rejected in turn.

The anecdote also underscores the *nonverbal* nature of the Intelligence. A solution to a problem can be constructed *before* it is articulated. In fact, the solution process may be totally invisible, even to the problem solver. This need not imply, however, that discoveries of this sort—the familiar "Aha!" phenomenon—are mysterious, intuitive, or unpredictable. The fact that it happens more frequently to some people (perhaps Nobel Prize winners) suggests the opposite. We interpret this as the work of the Logical-Mathematical Intelligence.

Along with the companion skill of language, logical-mathematical reasoning provides the basis for IQ tests. This form of Intelligence has been heavily investigated by traditional psychologists, and it is the archetype of "raw intelligence" or the problem-solving faculty that purportedly cuts across domains. It is perhaps ironic, then, that the actual mechanism by which one arrives at a solution to a logical-mathematical problem is not as yet properly understood.

This Intelligence is supported by our empirical criteria as well. Certain areas of the brain are more prominent in mathematical calculation than others. There are idiots savants who perform great feats of calculation even though they remain tragically deficient in most other areas. Child prodigies in mathematics abound. The development of this Intelligence in children has been carefully documented by Piaget and other psychologists.

Linguistic Intelligence

At the age of ten, T.S. Eliot created a magazine called "Fireside" to which he was the sole contributor. In a three-day period during his winter vacation, he created eight complete issues. Each one included poems, adventure stories, a gossip column, and humor. Some of this material survives and it displays the talent of the poet (see Soldo, 1982).

As with the Logical Intelligence, calling linguistic skill an "Intelligence" is consistent with the stance of traditional psychology. Linguistic Intelligence also passes our empirical tests. For instance, a specific area of the brain, called "Broca's Area," is responsible for the production of grammatical sentences. A person with damage to this area can understand words and sentences quite well but has difficulty putting them together in anything other than the simplest of sentences. At the same time, other thought processes may be entirely unaffected.

The gift of language is universal, and its development in children is strikingly constant across cultures. Even in deaf populations where a manual sign language is not explicitly taught, children will often "invent" their own manual language and use it surreptitiously! We thus see how an Intelligence may operate independently of a specific input modality or output channel.

Spatial Intelligence

Navigation around the Caroline Islands in the South Seas is accomplished without instruments. The position of the stars, as viewed from various islands, the weather patterns, and water color are the only sign posts. Each journey is broken into a series of segments; and the navigator learns the position of the stars within each of these segments. During the actual trip the navigator must envision mentally a reference island as it passes under a particular star and from that he computes the number of segments completed, the proportion of the trip remaining, and any corrections in heading that are required. The navigator cannot *see* the islands as he sails along; instead he maps their locations in his mental "picture" of the journey (Gardner, 1983).

Spatial problem solving is required for navigation and in the use of the notational system of maps. Other kinds of spatial problem solving are brought to bear in visualizing an object seen from a different angle and in playing chess. The visual arts also employ this Intelligence in the use of space.

Evidence from brain research is clear and persuasive. Just as the left hemisphere has, over the course of evolution, been selected as the site of linguistic processing, the right hemisphere proves to be the site most crucial for spatial processing. Damage to the right posterior regions causes impairment of the ability to find one's way around a site, to recognize faces or scenes, or to notice fine details.

Patients with damage specific to regions of the right hemisphere will attempt to compensate for their spatial deficits with linguistic strategies. They will try to reason aloud, to challenge the task, or even make up answers. But such nonspatial strategies are rarely successful.

Blind populations provide an illustration of the distinction between the Spatial Intelligence and visual perception. A blind person can recognize shapes by an indirect method: running a hand along the object translates into length of time of movement, which in turn is translated into the size of the object. For the blind person, the perceptual system of the tactile modality parallels the visual modality in the seeing person. The analogy between the spatial reasoning of the blind and the linguistic reasoning of the deaf is notable.

There are few child prodigies among visual artists, but there are idiots savants such as Nadia (Selfe, 1977). Despite a condition of severe autism, this preschool child made drawings of the most remarkable representational accuracy and finesse.

Interpersonal Intelligence

With little formal training in special education and nearly blind herself, Anne Sullivan began the intimidating task of instructing a blind and deaf seven-year-old Helen Keller. Sullivan's efforts at communication were complicated by the child's emotional struggle with the world around her. At their first meal together, this scene occurred:

Annie did not allow Helen to put her hand into Annie's plate and take what she wanted, as she had been accustomed to do with her family. It became a test of wills—hand thrust into plate, hand firmly put aside. The family, much upset, left the dining room. Annie locked the door and proceeded to eat her breakfast while Helen lay on the floor kicking and screaming, pushing and pulling at Annie's chair. [After half an hour] Helen went around the table looking for her family. She discovered no one else was there and that bewildered her. Finally, she sat down and began to eat her breakfast, but with her hands. Annie gave her a spoon. Down on the floor it clattered, and the contest of wills began anew (Lash, 1980, p. 52).

Anne Sullivan sensitively responded to the child's behavior. She wrote home: "The greatest problem I shall have to solve is how to discipline and control her without breaking her spirit. I shall go rather slowly at first and try to win her love."

In fact, the first "miracle" occurred two weeks later, well before the famous incident at the pumphouse. Annie had taken Helen to a small cottage near the family's house, where they could live alone. After seven days together, Helen's personality suddenly underwent a profound change—the therapy had worked:

My heart is singing with joy this morning. A miracle has happened! The wild little creature of two weeks ago has been transformed into a gentle child (p. 54).

It was just two weeks after this that the first breakthrough in Helen's grasp of language occurred; and from that point on, she progressed with incredible speed. The key to the miracle of language was Anne Sullivan's insight into the *person* of Helen Keller.

Interpersonal Intelligence builds on a core capacity to notice distinctions among others; in particular, contrasts in their moods, temperaments, motivations, and intentions. In more advanced forms, this Intelligence permits a skilled adult to read the intentions and desires of others, even when these have been hidden. This skill appears in a highly sophisticated form in religious or political leaders, teachers, therapists, and parents. The Helen Keller-Anne Sullivan story suggests that this Interpersonal Intelligence does not depend on language.

All indices in brain research suggest that the frontal lobes play a prominent role in interpersonal knowledge. Damage in this area can cause profound personality changes while leaving other forms of problem solving unharmed—a person is often "not the same person" after such an injury.

Alzheimer's disease, a form of presenile dementia, appears to attack posterior brain zones with a special ferocity, leaving spatial, logical, and linguistic computations severely imparied. Yet, Alzheimer patients will often remain well groomed, socially proper, and continually apologetic for their errors. In contrast, Pick's disease, another variety of presenile dementia that is more frontally oriented, creates a rapid loss of social graces.

Biological evidence for Interpersonal Intelligence encompasses two additional factors often cited as unique to humans. One factor is the prolonged childhood of primates, including the close attachment to the mother. In those cases where the mother is removed from early development, normal interpersonal development is in serious jeopardy. The second factor is the relative importance in humans of social interaction. Skills such as hunting, tracking, and killing in prehistoric societies required participation and cooperation of large numbers of people. The need for group cohesion, leadership, organization, and solidarity follows naturally from this.

Intrapersonal Intelligence

In an essay called "A Sketch of the Past," written almost as a diary entry, Virginia Woolf discusses the "cotton wool of existence"— the various mundane events of life. She contrasts this "cotton wool" with three specific and poignant memories from her childhood: a fight with her brother, seeing a particular flower in the garden, and hearing of the suicide of a past visitor:

These are three instances of exceptional moments. I often tell them over, or rather they come to the surface unexpectedly. But now for the first time I have written them down, and I realize something that I have never realized before. Two of these moments ended in a state of despair. The other ended, on the contrary, in a state of satisfaction.

The sense of horror (in hearing of the suicide) held me powerless. But in the case of the flower, I found a reason; and was thus able to deal with the sensation. I was not powerless.

Though I still have the peculiarity that I receive these sudden shocks, they are now always welcome; after the first surprise, I always feel instantly that they are particularly valuable. And so I go on to suppose that the shock-receiving capacity is what makes me a writer. I hazard the explanation that a shock is at once in my case followed by the desire to explain it. I feel that I have had a blow; but it is not, as I thought as a child, simply a blow from an enemy hidden behind the cotton wool of daily life; it is or will become a revelation of some order; it is a token of some real thing behind appearances; and I make it real by putting it into words (Woolf, 1976, pp. 69-70).

This quotation vividly illustrates the *Intrapersonal Intelligence*—knowledge of the internal aspects of a person: access to one's own feeling life, one's range of emotions, the capacity to effect discriminations among these emotions and eventually to label them and to draw upon them as a means of understanding and guiding one's own behavior. Since this Intelligence is the most private, it requires evidence from language, music, or some other more expressive form of Intelligence if the observer is to detect it at work. In the above quotation, for example, Linguistic Intelligence is drawn upon to convey intrapersonal knowledge; it embodies the interaction of Intelligences, a common phenomenon to which we will return later.

We see the familiar criteria at work in the Intrapersonal Intelligence. As with the Interpersonal Intelligence, the frontal lobes play a central role in personality change. Injury to the lower area of the frontal lobes is likely to produce irritability or euphoria; while injury to the higher regions is more likely to produce indifference, listlessness, slowness, and apathy—a kind of depressive personality. In such "frontal-lobe" individuals, the other cognitive functions often remain preserved. In contrast, among aphasics who have recovered sufficiently to describe their experiences, we find consistent testimony: while there may have been a diminution of general alertness and considerable depression about the condition, the individual in no way felt himself to be a different person. He recognized his own needs, wants, and desires and tried as best he could to achieve them.

The autistic child is a prototypical example of an individual with impaired Intrapersonal Intelligence; indeed, the child may not even be able to refer to himself. At the same time, such children often exhibit remarkable abilities in the musical, computational, spatial, or mechanical realms.

Evolutionary evidence for an Intrapersonal faculty is more difficult to come by, but we might speculate that the capacity to transcend
the satisfaction of instinctual drives is relevant. This becomes increasingly important in a species not perennially involved in the struggle
for survival.

In sum, then, both Interpersonal and Intrapersonal faculties pass
the tests of an Intelligence. They both feature problem-solving endeav-
ors with significance for the individual and the species. In the individual's sense of self, one encounters a melding of inter- and intra-per-
sonal components. Indeed, the sense of self emerges as one of the most
marvelous of human inventions—a symbol that represents all kinds of
information about a person and which is at the same time an invention
that all individuals construct for themselves.

Summary: The Unique Contributions of the Theory

As human beings, we all have a repertoire of skills for solving
different kinds of problems. Our investigation has begun, therefore,
with a consideration of these problems, the contexts they are found in,
and the culturally significant products that are the outcome. We have
not approached "intelligence" as a reified human faculty that is
brought to bear in literally any problem setting; rather, we have begun
with the problems that humans *solve* and worked back to the "Intelligences" that must be responsible.

Evidence from brain research, human development, evolution,
and cross-cultural comparisons was brought to bear in our search for
the relevant human Intelligences: a candidate was included only if
reasonable evidence to support its membership was found across these
diverse fields. Again, this tack differs from the traditional one: since
no candidate faculty is *necessarily* an Intelligence, we could choose on
a motivated basis. In the traditional approach to "intelligence," there
is no opportunity for this type of empirical decision.

We have also determined that these multiple human faculties, the
Intelligences, are to a significant extent *independent*. For example, research with brain-damaged adults repeatedly demonstrates that particular faculties can be lost while others are spared. This independence of Intelligences implies that a particularly high level of ability in
one Intelligence, say mathematics, does not require a similarly high
level in another Intelligence, like language or music. This independence of Intelligences contrasts sharply with traditional measures of
IQ that find high correlations among test scores. We speculate that
the usual correlations among subtests of IQ tests come about because

all of these tasks in fact measure the ability to respond rapidly to items of a logical-mathematical or linguistic sort; we believe that these correlations would be substantially reduced if one were to survey in a contextually appropriate way the full range of human problem-solving skills.

Until now, we have supported the fiction that adult roles depend largely on the flowering of a single Intelligence. In fact, however, nearly every cultural role of any degree of sophistication requires a combination of Intelligences. Thus, even an apparently straightforward role like playing the violin transcends a reliance on simple Musical Intelligence. To become a successful violinist requires bodily-kinesthetic dexterity and the interpersonal skills of relating to an audience and, in a different way, choosing a manager; quite possibly it involves an Intrapersonal Intelligence as well. Dance requires skills in Bodily-Kinesthetic, Musical, Interpersonal, and Spatial Intelligences in varying degrees. Politics requires an interpersonal skill, a linguistic facility, and perhaps some logical aptitude. Inasmuch as nearly every cultural role requires several Intelligences, it becomes important to consider individuals as a collection of aptitudes rather than as having a singular problem-solving faculty that can be measured directly through pencil-and-paper tests. Even given a relatively small number of such Intelligences, the diversity of human ability is created through the differences in these profiles. In fact, it may well be that the "total is greater than the sum of the parts." An individual may not be particularly gifted in any Intelligence; and yet, because of a particular combination or blend of skills, he or she may be able to fill some niche uniquely well. Thus it is of paramount importance to assess the particular combination of skills which may earmark an individual for a certain vocational or avocational niche.

Implications for Education

The theory of Multiple Intelligences was developed as an account of human cognition that can be subjected to empirical tests. The evidence for its educational utility has yet to be assembled. Nonetheless, the theory seems to harbor a number of educational implications that are worth consideration. In the following discussion we will begin by outlining what appears to be the natural developmental trajectory of an Intelligence. Turning then to aspects of education, we will comment on the role of nurturing and explicit instruction in this development. From this analysis we find that assessment of Intelligences can play a crucial role in curriculum development.

The Natural Growth of an Intelligence: A Developmental Trajectory

Since all Intelligences are part of the human genetic heritage; at some basic level each Intelligence is manifested universally, independent of education and cultural support. Exceptional populations aside for the moment, *all* humans possess certain core abilities in each of the Intelligences.

The natural trajectory of development in each Intelligence begins with *raw patterning ability*, for example, the ability to make tonal differentiations in Musical Intelligence or to appreciate three-dimensional arrangements in Spatial Intelligence. These abilities appear universally; they may also appear at a heightened level in that part of the population that is "at promise" in that domain. The "raw" Intelligence predominates during the first year of life.

Intelligences are glimpsed through different lenses at subsequent points in development. In the subsequent stage, the Intelligence is encountered through a *symbol system*: language is encountered through sentences and stories, music through songs, spatial understanding through drawings, bodily-kinesthetic through gesture or dance, and so on. At this point children demonstrate their abilities in the various Intelligences through their grasp of various symbol systems. Yehudi Menuhin's response to the sound of the violin illustrates the Musical Intelligence of a gifted individual coming in contact with a particular aspect of the symbol system.

As development progresses, each Intelligence together with its accompanying symbol system is represented in a *notational system*. Mathematics, mapping, reading, music notation, and so on, are second-order symbol systems in which the marks on paper come to stand for symbols. In our culture, these notational systems are typically mastered in a formal educational setting.

Finally, during adolescence and adulthood, the Intelligences are expressed through the range of *vocational or avocational pursuits*. For example, the Logical-Mathematical Intelligence, that began as sheer pattern ability in infancy and developed through symbolic mastery of early childhood and the notations of the school years, achieves mature expression in such roles as mathematician, accountant, scientist, cashier. Similarly, the Spatial Intelligence passes from the mental maps of the infant, to the symbolic operations required in drawings and the notational systems of maps, to the adult roles of navigator, chess player, or topologist.

Although all humans partake of each Intelligence to some degree, certain individuals are said to be "at promise." They are highly endowed with the core abilities and skills of that Intelligence. This fact becomes important for the culture as a whole, since, in general, these exceptionally gifted individuals will make notable advances in the cultural manifestations of that Intelligence. It is not important that *all* members of the Puluwat tribe demonstrate precocious spatial abilities needed for navigation by the stars, nor is it necessary for all Westerners to master mathematics to the degree necessary to make a significant contribution to theoretical physics. So long as the individuals "at promise" in particular domains are located efficiently, the overall knowledge of the group will be advanced in all domains.

While some individuals are "at promise" in an Intelligence, others are "at risk." In the absence of special aids, those at risk in an Intelligence will be most likely to fail tasks involving that Intelligence. Conversely, those at promise will be most likely to succeed. It may be that intensive intervention at an early age can bring a larger number of children to an "at promise" level

The special developmental trajectory of an individual at promise varies with Intelligence. Thus, mathematics and music are characterized by the early appearance of gifted children who perform relatively early at or near an adult level. In contrast, the Linguistic and Personal Intelligences appear to arise much more gradually; prodigies are rare. Moreover, mature performance in one area does not imply mature performance in another area, just as gifted achievement in one does not imply gifted achievement in another.

Implications of the Developmental Trajectory for Education

Because the Intelligences are manifested in different ways at different developmental levels, both assessment and nurturing need to occur in apposite ways. What nurtures in infancy would be inappropriate at later stages, and vice versa. In the preschool and early elementary years, instruction should emphasize opportunity. It is during these years that children can discover something of their own peculiar interests and abilities. In the cases of very talented children, such discoveries often happen by themselves through spontaneous "crystallizing experiences" (Walters and Gardner, 1984). For others, specifically designed encounters with materials, equipment, or other people can help instigate such discovery of one's own métier.

During the school-age years, some mastery of notational systems is essential in our society. The self-discovery environment of early schooling cannot provide the structure needed for the mastery of specific notational systems like the sonata form or algebra. In fact, during this period some tutelage is needed by virtually all children. One problem is to find the right form, since group tutelage can be helpful in some instances and harmful in others. Another problem is to orchestrate the connection between practical knowledge and the knowledge embodied in symbolic systems and notational systems.

Finally, in adolescence, most students must be assisted in their choice of careers. This task is made more complex by the manner in which Intelligences interact in many cultural roles. For instance, being a doctor certainly requires Logical-Mathematical Intelligence; but general practice demands a strong interpersonal skill while surgery requires a bodily-kinesthetic dexterity. Internships, apprenticeships, and involvement with the actual materials of the cultural role become critical at this point in development.

Several implications for explicit instruction can be drawn from this analysis. First, the role of instruction in relation to the manifestation of an Intelligence changes across the developmental trajectory. The enriched environment appropriate for the younger years is less relevant for adolescents. Conversely, explicit instruction in the notational system, appropriate for older children, is largely inappropriate for younger ones.

Explicit instruction must be evaluated in light of the developmental trajectories of the Intelligences. Students benefit from explicit instruction only if the information or training fits into their specific place on the developmental progression. A particular kind of instruction can be either too early at one point or too late at another. For example, Suzuki training in music pays little attention to the notational system, while providing a great deal of support or scaffolding for learning the fine points of instrumental technique. While this emphasis may be very powerful for training preschool children, it can produce stunted musical development when imposed at a late point on the developmental trajectory. Such a highly structured instructional environment can accelerate progress and produce a larger number of children "at promise," but in the end it may ultimately limit choices and inhibit self-expression.

An exclusive focus on linguistic and logical skills in formal schooling can shortchange individuals with skills in other Intelligences. It is evident from inspection of adult roles, even in language-dominated Western society, that spatial, interpersonal, bodily-kinesthetic skills often play key roles. Yet linguistic and logical skills form the core of most diagnostic tests of "Intelligence" and are placed on a pedagogical pedestal in our schools.

The Large Need: Assessment

The general pedagogical program described here presupposes accurate understanding of the profile of Intelligences of the individual learner. Such a careful assessment procedure allows informed choices about careers and avocations. It also permits a more enlightened search for remedies for difficulties. Assessment of deficiencies can predict difficulties the learner will have; moreover, it can suggest alternative routes to an educational goal (learning mathematics via spatial relations; learning music through linguistic techniques).

Assessment, then, becomes a central feature of an educational system. Until now, we have blithely assumed that such assessment can be made. In truth, however, the assessment of intellectual profiles remains a task for the future. We believe that we will need to depart from standardized testing. We also believe that standard pencil-and-paper short-answer tests sample only a small proportion of intellectual abilities and often reward a certain kind of decontextualized facility. The means of assessment we favor should ultimately search for genuine problem-solving or product-fashioning skills in individuals across a range of materials.

An assessment of a particular Intelligence (or set of Intelligences) should highlight problems that can be solved *in the materials of that Intelligence*. That is, mathematical assessment should present problems in mathematical settings. For younger children, these could consist of Piagetian-style problems in which talk is kept to a minimum. For older children, derivation of proofs in a novel numerical system might suffice. In music, on the other hand, the problems would be embedded in a musical system. Younger children could be asked to assemble tunes from individual musical segments. Older children could be shown how to compose a rondo or fugue from simple patterns.

An important aspect of assessing Intelligences must include the individual's ability to solve problems or create products using the materials of the intellectual medium. Equally important, however, is the determination of which Intelligence is favored when an individual has a choice. One technique for getting at this proclivity is to expose the individual to a sufficiently complex situation that can stimulate several Intelligences; or to provide a set of materials drawn from different Intelligences and determine toward which one an individual gravitates and how deeply he or she explores it.

As an example, consider what happens when a child sees a complex film in which several Intelligences figure prominently: music, people interacting, a maze to be solved, or a particular bodily skill, may all compete for attention. Subsequent "debriefing" with the child should reveal the features to which the child paid attention; these will be related to the profile of Intelligences in that child. Or consider a situation in which children are taken into a room with several different kinds of equipment and games. Simple measures of the regions in which children spend time and the kinds of activities they engage in should yield insights into the individual child's profile of Intelligence.

Tests of this sort differ in two important ways from the traditional measures of "intelligence." First, they rely on materials, equipment, interviews, and so on to generate the problems to be solved; this contrasts with the traditional pencil-and-paper measures used in intelligence testing. Second, results are reported as part of an individual profile of intellectual propensities, rather than as a single index of intelligence or rank within the population. In contrasting strengths and weaknesses, they can suggest options for future learning.

Scores are not enough. This assessment procedure should suggest to parents, teachers, and, eventually, to children themselves, the sorts of activities that are available at home, in school, or in the wider community. Drawing on this information, children can bolster their own particular sets of intellectual weaknesses or combine their intellectual strengths in a way that is satisfying vocationally and avocationally.

Coping with the Plurality of Intelligences

Under the Multiple Intelligences theory, an Intelligence can serve both as the *content* of instruction and the *means* or medium for communicating that content. This state of affairs has important ramifications for instruction. For example, suppose that a child is learning some mathematical principle but is not skilled in Logical-Mathematical Intelligence. That child will probably experience some difficulty during the learning process. The reason for the difficulty is straightforward: the mathematical principle to be learned (the content) exists only in the logical-mathematical world and it ought to be communicated through mathematics (the medium). That is, the mathematical principle cannot be translated *entirely* into words (which is a linguistic medium) or spatial models (a spatial medium). At some point in the learning process, the mathematics of the principle must "speak for itself." In our present case, it is at just this level that the learner experiences difficulty—the learner (who is not especially "mathematical") and the problem (which is very much "mathematical") are not in accord. Mathematics, as a *medium*, has failed.

Although this situation is a necessary conundrum in light of Multiple Intelligences theory, we can propose various solutions. In the present example, the teacher must attempt to find an alternative route to the mathematical content—a metaphor in another medium. Language is perhaps the most obvious alternative, but spatial modeling and even a bodily-kinesthetic metaphor may prove appropriate in some cases. In this way, the student is given a *secondary* route to the solution to the problem, perhaps through the medium of an Intelligence that is relatively strong for that individual.

Two features of this hypothetical scenario must be stressed. First, in such cases, the secondary route—the language, spatial model, or whatever—is at best a metaphor or translation. It is not mathematics itself. And at some point, the learner must translate back into the domain of mathematics. Without this translation, what is learned tends to remain at a relatively superficial level; cookbook-style mathematical performance results from following instructions (linguistic translation) without understanding why (mathematics re-translation).

Second, the alternative route is not guaranteed. There is no *necessary* reason why a problem in one domain *must be translatable* into a metaphorical problem in another domain. Successful teachers find these translations with relative frequency; but as learning becomes more complex, the likelihood of a successful translation diminishes.

While Multiple Intelligences theory is consistent with much empirical evidence, it has not been subjected to strong experimental tests within psychology. Within the area of education, the applications of the theory are even more tentative and speculative. Our hunches will have to be revised many times in light of actual classroom experience. Still there are important reasons for considering the theory of Multiple Intelligences and its implications for education. First of all, it is clear that many talents, if not Intelligences, are overlooked nowadays; individuals with these talents are the chief casualties of the single-minded, single-funneled approach to the mind. There are many unfilled or poorly filled niches in our society and it would be opportune to guide individuals with the right set of abilities to these billets. Finally, our world is beset with problems; to have any chance of solving them, we must make the very best use of the Intelligences we possess. Perhaps recognizing the plurality of Intelligences and the manifold ways in which human individuals may exhibit them is an important first step.

References

Connor, A. *Voices from Cooperstown*. New York: Collier Books, 1982. (Based on a quotation taken from *The Babe Ruth Story*, New York: E.P. Dutton, 1948).

Gallwey, T. *Inner Tennis*. New York: Random House, 1976.

Gardner, H. *Frames of Mind*. New York: Basic Books, 1976.

Keller, E. *A Feeling for the Organism*. Salt Lake City: W.H. Freeman, 1983.

Lash, J. *Helen and Teacher: The Story of Helen Keller and Anne Sullivan Macy*. New York: Delacorte Press, 1980.

Menuhin, Y. *Unfinished Journey*. New York: Alfred Knopf, 1977.

Selfe, L. *Nadia: A Case of Extraordinary Drawing Ability in an Autistic Child*. New York: Academic Press, 1977.

Soldo, J. "Jovial Juvenilia: T.S. Eliot's First Magazine." *Biography* 5 (1982): 25-37.

Walters, J., and Gardner, H. "Crystallizing Experiences: Discovering an Intellectual Gift." In *Studies in Giftedness*. Edited by R. Sternberg and J. Davidson. Cambridge: University Press, 1984.

Woolf, V. *Moments of Being*. Sussex: The University Press, 1976.

2. Intellectual Development of the Gifted

A. Harry Passow

EFFORTS TO NURTURE GIFTED INDIVIDUALS HAVE A VERY LONG HISTORY, dating back thousands of years and existing in many different cultures. Over the years, concepts of giftedness have varied, as have attitudes toward gifted individuals. School involvement in the identification and nurturing of giftedness is a relatively new phenomenon, just as formal schooling is a relatively recent idea. In the United States, from the time when William T. Harris instituted rapid, flexible promotion in the St. Louis Public Schools in 1868 as a way of providing for more able pupils, a variety of efforts have been made to identify, nurture, and "meet the needs" of *pupils of supernormal ability, rapid learners, high achievers, brilliant children, gifted*, and a variety of other terms and labels—all of which have been used to designate individuals with high intelligence and/or high achievement. In 1955, Newland (1955) found no fewer than 51 different terms used to characterize "gifted populations" in 126 research reports. This diversity reflects the absence of a single, uniform conception of giftedness guiding the efforts of either researchers or practitioners.

All aspects of identification and development of the gifted depend on the underlying conception of the nature of giftedness. This view is

Author's note: I gratefully acknowledge the assistance of my colleague, Abraham J. Tannenbaum, in the preparation of this chapter.

reflected in the discussion of the intellectual development of the gifted that follows because it is based on a particular point of view. For example, we believe that intellectually gifted children are hardly ever gifted at all except by childhood standards. They may distinguish themselves among age mates, but if their performance or productive skills do not continue to grow at an accelerated pace as they mature through adolescence and approach adulthood, they will lapse into mediocrity. There are examples, such as the case of a Mozart or a Mendelssohn, when children excel even by universal adult standards, but these are rare exceptions to the rule. What educators and psychologists recognize as giftedness in children is really *potential* giftedness, which denotes promise rather than fulfillment and probabilities rather than certainties about future accomplishments. How high these probabilities are in any given case depends on the match between a child's budding talents and the kinds of nurturance provided.

A Proposed Definition of Giftedness

One way to look at giftedness is to think of two varieties of potentially gifted children: those who have it in them to become exemplary *producers* of ideas and those who show early signs of becoming critically acclaimed *performers*, serving audiences or individual clients. Both types of giftedness operate in spheres of activity that enhance the moral, physical, emotional, social, intellectual, or aesthetic life of humanity.

Outstanding contributors to the arts, sciences, letters, and general well-being of fellow humans tend often to show signs of promise in childhood. It is, therefore, reasonable to identify precocious children as the pool from which the most highly gifted are likely to emerge. But precocity may only signify just the rapid learning of ideas, the ability to grasp abstractions quickly and efficiently, and the mastery of skills far beyond those expected at the child's age level. Early schooling is reserved mainly for such emphases on content absorption as it involves encountering, distilling, synthesizing, and *consuming* knowledge. *Producing* knowledge with great inventiveness and impact—a sign of giftedness—comes later in an individual's growth cycle, but the discerning parent or educator can see signs of it long before it reaches fruition.

Similarly, the gifted performer has abilities and temperament that have incubated over the years, although they may be difficult to recognize in their early stages. I use the term *performance* here to include far more than just staged entertainment in the concert hall or theater. It also encompasses a variety of high-level service skills such as medical assistance, social and psychological treatment, teaching, and many other areas. Those who qualify as gifted performers are capable of attracting widespread appreciation when they demonstrate their abilities. Excluded are the amateurs who are able to perform (but not brilliantly) and those who simply appreciate the performance of others.

As Tannenbaum has suggested, five broad conditions account for a person's giftedness: (1) superior general intellect, (2) distinctive special aptitudes, (3) the right blending of nonintellectual traits, (4) a challenging environment, and (5) the smile of good fortune at crucial periods of life. A discussion of intellective determinants is necessarily limiting, therefore, because it encompasses only the first two of the five determinants. In reality, each of these facilitators is necessary, though not sufficient, for achieving excellence in any area of activity. Thus, no combination of four qualifiers is adequate to compensate for the absence or inadequacy of the fifth, and the minimal essentials, or threshold levels, for all five vary with every talent domain. For example, giftedness in theoretical physics requires high intelligence and fewer interpersonal skills than does giftedness in social service professions. Obviously, then, no single set of measurement criteria can be equally effective for identifying, say, potential scientists and politicians. Nor is it meaningful to suggest that either the scientist or the politician is the "smarter" of the two because of the differences in their general intelligence or in their special aptitudes. The five factors interact in different ways for separate talent domains, but they are all represented in some way in every form of giftedness (Tannenbaum, 1983).

Some argue for adding superior "creativity" as a sixth condition for attaining individual excellence. The problem is that listing creativity would give the impression that it is separable from the five factors rather than closely identified with all of them. In fact, creativity is synonymous with giftedness, defined here as the potential for becoming either an outstanding producer or performer, not just a consumer, spectator, or amateur appreciator of ideas. To the best of our knowledge, creativity (or giftedness) consists of a not-yet-known combination of general and specific abilities and personality traits associated with high potential that can be realized in a stimulating environment with the help of good fortune.

Creativity (or giftedness) is judged by two criteria: the extent and quality of its innovativeness. Often measures of "creativity" naively concentrate on off-beat and prolific responses to problems as suitable criteria, while neglecting the aesthetic brilliance of these responses and forgetting that what is rare is not necessarily valued. Because it denotes rare *and* valued human accomplishment, creativity should be conceptualized as interchangeable with giftedness. After all, giftedness is reflected in the ability to be an innovator of what is new and treasurable, not just a curator of what is old and treasured.

General Intellect and Giftedness

The power center for giftedness is the human brain, which controls both the magnitude and diversity of individual potential. It can transport an Einstein into heights of abstraction and a da Vinci into flights of creativity that are so far beyond ordinary accomplishments as to seem almost miraculous. It can also generate nearly endless traces of genius, ranging from the esoterica of plasma physics, to the visual spectacle of the Taj Mahal, to the magical cadences of a Miltonic sonnet, to the sublime sounds of an *Eroica* symphony, to the gustatory delights of gourmet cooking, to the intricate beauties of Oriental knot designs, and on and on into every possible domain of individual activity.

To date, a great deal more is known about the extent of human intellectual strength than about the essence of human intellect. Thus, much of the literature has referred to gifted children in terms of their *high intelligence.* But the meaning of this term as it applies to such children is not much clearer today than it was more than a half-century ago when Boring defined intelligence as something that is measured by tests of intelligence. However, those who view giftedness from a psychological perspective are well aware that scores on tests of intelligence are intended to provide clues rather than understandings about superior potential.

As tenuous as it is to define and describe giftedness fulfilled, it is even more precarious to speak with assurance about it in its period of promise, when predictions have to be made about a child's future development. Yet, studying high-level potential among school-age children and youth is of obvious interest and concern to educators, because the development of appropriate programs and provisions for nurturing that potential is what schools are about.

The largest-scale test of the hypothesis that there is a development linkage between identification as prediction of giftedness and its nurturance leading to superior performance can be found in the so-called *Genetic Studies of Genius,* begun in 1922 by Lewis M. Terman and his associates and continued at present by Pauline and Robert Sears.

Terman's basic argument was that greatness does not reflect a mysterious, freakish mutation but stems from an extraordinary ability to exercise sensitive judgment in solving problems, to adapt to new situations, and to learn from performing various tasks and experiencing various situations. Terman believed that all people have these abilities in various degrees but that the gifted excel in them and are, therefore, most successful in measuring up to the demands of school and society. Moreover, Terman believed that these mental traits can be captured in an IQ score early in life and that the gifted are those who rate in the highest percentile on such measures. So confident was Terman in equating giftedness with high IQ that he asserted at the outset that it would be from the ranks of children of high IQ, and from nowhere else, that geniuses in every line of endeavor would come.

From the vast amount of data collected regularly since 1922, some of the original expectations Terman had have been verified and other remain doubtful. One enduring legacy is Terman's insistence that giftedness can be recognized in a continuum of abilities possessed by all people. He saw the gifted and the nongifted as having the same organization of abilities but differing in the extent to which they are capable of cultivating some of them. Thus, Terman assumed difference in degree rather than in kind. Acceptance of this assumption means that studies of the nature of and measurement of gifted performance can be subsumed under general investigation of human mentality.

Another outcome of Terman's work is his conclusion that potential giftedness reveals itself even in childhood. The once popular platitude, "Early ripe, early rot" has been turned into a canard by the Terman studies. There are, of course, many instances of failure to fulfill predicted potential, but these are exceptions to the rule that children with ample mental abilities, reasonably stable personalities, and proper nurturance tend eventually to excel in their careers, given the right opportunities to exhibit excellence. And, because giftedness seldom materializes suddenly and unaccountably in adulthood, but has its roots in its early years of growth, schools are in a key position to help gifted children realize their potential. The findings suggest a need for special educational opportunities for the gifted, an idea that would be irrelevant were there no developmental connection between early promise and later fulfillment.

Some of the conclusions reached by Terman have not fared equally well. Besides initiating what has become an endless debate over the value of IQ measures in distinguishing between gifted and nongifted children, Terman contributed at least two ideas that have since fallen into disfavor. The first has to do with the consistency of IQ scores and the idea that giftedness is basically a hereditary phenomenon. Ample evidence from other major longitudinal studies shows dramatic shifts in IQ among individual children. The second has to do with his apparent belief in the indivisibility of the organization of mental powers. Although Terman never pretended to advocate a theory of intelligence, his need for a single score to measure potential giftedness, and the way he obtained it, implied an assumption that intelligence consists of one general factor. Later studies have demonstrated that mental powers are more likely multifaceted, consisting of special aptitudes that seem to be distinguishable from each other, not part of a single, overall intellectual power.

The Terman longitudinal study—more than 60 years old now—has been criticized on a variety of bases, including the selection procedures, the criteria on which adult attainments have been judged, and the lack of minority subjects. Whatever faults and shortcomings they may have, the studies must be considered as landmark longitudinal research that has provided significant insights into intellectual development, not only of the gifted. There has been much speculation about what would have happened to Terman's female subjects had they grown up in the current era of more equal opportunities.

One of the major problems in understanding giftedness as it develops over the lifespan is that much of the research literature equates it with high IQ. Many modern writers on the subject deny that association as too simplistic but often ignore their own denials by generalizing about giftedness on the basis of studies of high-IQ children. It is not easy to avoid such a trap, because much of the published research has been conducted on this kind of population.

Followers of the Terman tradition define giftedness as general intellectual superiority that the individual channels into one of many possible areas of specialization on the basis of personal interests, encounters with inspiring teachers, or encouraging job opportunities. For purposes of locating such a pool of potentially gifted children who are too young to choose specific life careers, there is no single, more valid measure than the IQ. Others srongly disagree with the tendency to equate giftedness with IQ. For example, Robinson (1977) argues that:

In the post-Terman era, it has indeed become possible to become a "gifted" individual without having any noticeable gift at all. We routinely categorize children as "gifted" if their IQ scores are above 125, 130, 140 or whatever cutoff score we happen to choose, in spite of the fact that they do not do better than average work in school or demonstrate in any other fashion an exceptional degree of talent (p. 2).

Generally speaking, the movement away from exclusive reliance on IQ and its correlates to define giftedness is not intended simply to devalue the IQ. Instead, the argument is that IQ limits giftedness to traditional academics and is not helpful in distinguishing among different kinds of intellectual and artistic functioning. Taylor and Ellison (1975), for example, point out that intelligence tests encompass only about eight intellectual talents, which represent a small fraction of the well over a hundred that are known to exist. Taylor and Ellison have proposed a "multiple talent" approach to seek out children who are not only learners and reproducers but also thinkers, producers, decision makers, communicators, forecasters, and creators.

So influential has been the multiple-talent approach to defining giftedness that it was incorporated into a federal policy statement in the so-called Marland Report (1971):

Gifted and talented children are those identified by professionally qualified persons who by virtue of outstanding abilities are capable of high performance . . . .

Children capable of high performance include those with demonstrated achievement and/or potential ability in any of the following areas, singly or in combination:
  1. general intellectual ability;
  2. specific academic aptitude;
  3. creative or productive thinking;
  4. leadership ability;
  5. visual and performing arts;
  6. psychomotor ability.

Although the federal definition has been popular in schools throughout the country and has served, as Renzulli (1978) noted, "the very useful purpose of calling attention to a wider variety of abilities that should be included in a definition of giftedness," it also has presented some major problems. Renzulli points to the omission of non-intellective factors that are vital in characterizing giftedness, such as task commitment and persistence; to the nonparallel nature of the categories, some of which deal with cognitive processes and others with accomplished performance; and to the tendency for practitioners to treat the six categories as if they were independent of one another, resulting in separate identification procedures for each category.

The use of factor analysis to demonstrate the existence of distinguishable special abilities was originally developed by Thurstone (1947), whose work led him eventually to identify seven primary factors that can be recognized as separate entities, though they partially relate to each other as well as to an overall g (general) factor. These include verbal meaning, word fluency, number ability, memory, spatial relations, perceptual speed, and reasoning ability.

A more elaborate use of factor analysis techniques led Guilford (1959, 1967) to develop his "Structure of Intellect" model, which denotes the possibilities of as many as 150 separate abilities in human beings. The Structure of Intellect model is usually presented in the form of a cube with its three faces showing three different dimensions: *operations* (cognition, memory, divergent production, convergent production, and evaluation), *content* (figural/visual, figural/auditory, symbolic, semantic, and behavioral), and *products* (units, classes, relations, systems, transformations, and implications). Operations denotes the alternative ways in which the individual can process any kind of informational content and develop out of it products that take any form. Divergent production of semantic systems, for example, denotes the ability to produce a variety of ideas from a known set of units.

Structure of Intellect has been developed into an "instructional program" aimed at nurturing the various mental abilities, particularly in programs for the gifted. The factors remain to be tested fully for their concurrent and predictive validity. It may be that none of the factor measures correlates with accomplishment in a specific line of activity any more than does a test of general intelligence. It may even turn out that a small handful of subtests in the battery developed by Guilford provides a good estimate of IQ, as do the Verbal Reasoning and Numerical Ability subtests of the Differential Aptitude Tests. It should be kept in mind, however, that Guilford never intended to compete with the IQ in measuring human potential but rather meant to define the variety and organization of human abilities. He attempted to show mental functioning as represented by an aggregate of special competencies that can be discerned and described. Such a conceptual framework is especially valuable for the educator who wants a clear perspective on the range of special aptitudes that ought to be cultivated at school and who also wants to inventory those that are and are not neglected. In all probability, only a few of the abilities receive more than passing attention in any curriculum, even those for the gifted.

Of all the "operations" in the Structure of Intellect, the one that has received widest attention has been divergent production, which Guilford and his followers have related closely to the concept of creativity. Divergent thinking tests are currently used widely to identify "highly creative children," based on the assumption that such tests reveal special talents in children that would ordinarily be overlooked by the IQ. Some studies support the validity of such tests, whereas others do not.

In what was probably the longest-range and largest-scale study of divergent thinking aptitudes, Torrance (1981) followed up pupils from two elementary schools who had been tested using *Torrance Tests of Creative Thinking* some 21 to 25 years earlier. Data on adolescent and creative behavior were obtained from 211 of the 400 pupils originally tested. Subjects who had high scores during childhood reported relatively impressive numbers of high school and post-high school achievements and "creative style of life" accomplishments that had not been recognized publicly. Torrance's students also assigned superior ratings to the subjects on the quality of their highest creative achievements as well as the quality of their career aspirations and images.

Because there are few longitudinal studies of predicting and assessing adult creative accomplishments, Torrance's (1975) earlier reflections on the predictive validity of divergent thinking tests seem still appropriate:

When confronted by the fact that creative functioning involves a variety of phenomena which occur simultaneously and interact with one another, how much weight should we expect measures of general creative abilities to carry? Research evidence indicates that the motivation of the subject, his early life experiences, the immediate and long-range rewards, the richness of the environment, and other factors are all important enough to make a difference in creative functioning and furthermore that these phenomena interact with one another.

The relatively recent research on the hemispheres of the brain has been studied for implications for the development and education of the gifted. Studies have indicated that there are separate and independent functions for each brain hemisphere. The left hemisphere is believed to control logical and analytic thought processes, including speaking, writing, and mathematical calculations. The right hemisphere, on the other hand, is believed to control creative and artistic thinking, spatial relationships, and music comprehension.

Some educators of the gifted have examined ways of using this emerging body of knowledge about the brain and its functioning in teaching and learning. As Clark (1979) has observed, for example:

More important than recognizing the specialization of hemispheres is the evidence of the need for interaction and intersupport between the hemispheres . . . . Without the support of a well-developed right hemisphere, such left brain growth will be inhibited. For years, good teachers and parents have intuitively used both right and left brain functions in their teaching. The evidence for specialization now validates their teaching idea (p. 359).

Over the years, as research has been conducted on understanding the nature and maturation of superior abilities and talents, more and more questions have been raised about the processes involved as more and more light has been shed on those processes. There is as yet no widespread accepted theory of giftedness, although there is a considerable body of knowledge about individual differences and their nurture. As Read (1982) has put it, "Few researchers have managed to capture the amazing convergence of biological, social, cultural, and psychological factors that characterize the expression of exceptional talent. Even less common are longitudinal investigations that track the course of these talents from their first flowering in childhood to mature expression in a productive and creative career" (p. 2). The lifelong tracking of Terman's subjects is what makes that study so unique and important, even though it has not provided definitive answers to all of the questions about talent development.

Feldman (1982) has argued "that the traditional emphasis on precocious test performance, however productive, has had an unfortunate tendency to narrow the focus of the field, leaving outside its borders many interesting research questions" (p. 5). Feldman advocates using findings from the developmental sciences—psychology, biology, brain research, epistemology, and literature—to stimulate and guide work to better understand giftedness and creativity.

Renzulli (1980) has observed that "In spite of vast amounts of research on every conceivable aspect of the learning process, we still have difficulty pinpointing the reasons for the remarkable differences in learning efficiency and creativity among persons with similar genetic and environmental experiences . . . . We simply do not know" (p. 601).

Although there is much that we do not know about the development of giftedness, we have learned a good deal about the nature and nurture of giftedness. Much of what we do know is related to school performance and academic achievement, as well as to the performance and behavior of adults who are recognized as gifted. We know, for example, that compared with what Terman called "the generality," gifted individuals learn more rapidly, learn qualitatively differently, achieve and use higher-order cognitive skills more readily, demonstrate creative expression more often, exhibit critical thinking and problem-solving capabilities, exhibit greater self-direction and independence, tend to be more reflective and insightful, evidence greater persistence and task commitment, and display unusual precocity in some areas. Their unusual potential is manifested in degree rather than kind and in precocity. It is these differentials in potential and performance that have provided guidance for educators of the gifted.

Differentiated Curriculum and Instruction

For more than a century, schools have provided programs aimed at nurturing the potential of gifted children and youth. As the Marland Report (1971) put it, the gifted "are children who require differentiated educational programs and/or services beyond those normally provided by the regular school program in order to realize their contribution to self and society" (p. 2). The phrase "beyond those normally provided by the regular school program" implies that there is a regular curriculum that is to be enriched or accelerated for the gifted. Most programs and provisions for the gifted have applied this concept of enriching or accelerating the educational experiences and opportunities for the gifted; few have developed what Dishart (1980) argued for—"curricula which are enriched enough and accelerated enough for gifted learners [in the first place]" (p. 26).

In designing differentiated curriculums and instruction for the gifted, all elements of the process are subject to differentiation—the goals and objectives, the content, the teaching–learning strategies, the resources, the organization of learners, the organization of time and space, and the means for evaluation.

Whereas the basic goal for the education of the gifted is the same as that for all children—that is, fullest development of individual potential—genuine differences in school experiences are only designed as specific goals are clarified. What educational imperatives are there for the gifted? If giftedness is something relative and qualitative rather than discrete and quantitative, what are the essential learnings for individuals who have been identified as potentially gifted? Are there essential learnings that the gifted must experience if they are to achieve maximum self-realization and fulfill their potential? The question of appropriate goals and objectives for the diverse population identified as gifted poses a number of issues and problems for educational planners.

The general education curriculum is a basic, common curriculum in which the knowledge, skills, insights, values, and attitudes that are required of all individuals to function optimally in society are nurtured and developed. The general education involves, as Ward (1961) has put it, "those experiences serviceable in educating and training common higher mental processes . . . such as reasoning, judgment, abstraction, and understanding per se" (p. 35). The common curriculum provides the substantive content as well as the cognitive and intuitive processes individuals need to function as "consumers" in society and on which the specialized curricular experiences can build for individuals to function as "producers."

There is some consensus regarding the general nature of the general education curriculum for the development of the gifted. For example, the Curriculum Council of the National/State Leadership Training Institute for the Gifted/Talented (Passow, 1982) has proposed some guiding principles for curriculum differentiation for gifted children. They include the following:

1. The content of curricula for the gifted/talented should focus on and be organized to include more elaborate, complex, and in-depth study of major ideas, problems, and themes that integrate knowledge with and across systems of thought.

2. Curricula for gifted/talented should allow for the development and application of productive thinking skills to enable students to reconceptualize existing knowledge and generate new knowledge.

3. Curricula for the gifted/talented should enable them to explore constantly changing knowledge and information and develop the attitude that knowledge is worth pursuing in an open world.

4. Curricula for the gifted/talented should encourage exposure to selection, and use of appropriate and specialized resources.

5. Curricula for the gifted/talented should promote self-initiated and self-directed learning and growth.

6. Curricula for the gifted/talented should provide for the development of self-understandings and the understandings of one's relationship to persons, societal institutions, nature and culture.

7. Evaluation of curricula for the gifted/talented should be conducted in accordance with the prior stated principles, stressing higher-level skills, creativity, and excellence in performance and products (pp. 7-10).

There is a specialized curriculum aimed at nurturing the special talent areas of the individual, which consists of learning engagements and opportunities that enable the individual to identify and develop the skills, knowledge, insights, values, and understandings needed to realize one's area of specialized talent potential.

For either the general/common curriculum or the specialized curriculum, educational experiences and learning opportunities may be differentiated in at least three ways: in breadth and/or depth, in tempo or pace, or in kind or nature. Different disciplines and content and different processes lend themselves to curricular adaptations differently.

The education planner faces questions as to what should be the balance between the general/common curriculum and the specialized curriculum. Normally, as children progress through school, the emphasis and the amount of time devoted to the general curriculum tend to decrease as the amount of time devoted to specialized education increases. What subjects, what disciplines, what learning opportunities are appropriate for gifted children? In most schools, the elementary curriculum is most likely to consist of a common curriculum for all, with some effort to adjust, modify, or differentiate the curriculum to accommodate individual differences. At that level, some programs aim at beginning to nurture special talents, often by providing opportunities for nurturing a special interest or even by identifying special aptitudes. Unless the ability or aptitude is especially outstanding, the specialized curriculum tends to be exploratory and experimental when targeted for younger ages. Opportunities for creative writing, computer study, more advanced science or mathematics, archeology, and so forth, may be provided for gifted children. In the early years, however, the purpose is not that of developing writers, computer programmers, scientists, archeologists, and so forth. At the elementary school level, these kinds of learning opportunities and engagements are designed to enable gifted children to explore their own interests and begin to nurture their potential in particular areas of ability and aptitude.

At the secondary level, the issue of balance between the general/common curriculum and the specialized curriculum is sharpened. There is agreement that gifted individuals usually require postsecondary or professional training if their potential is to be realized and that one of the purposes of secondary schools is to provide the base for such further education. How much specialized education and what kind of balance should be maintained with general education are questions on which there is not always consensus. Some argue that schools should offer the gifted neither vocational nor preprofessional education but only the broadest kind of general education, and that the common curriculum—most often that which constitutes the college-preparatory program—is most appropriate for gifted youth. They assume that it is at the tertiary or higher education levels that specialization appropriate to the development of high-level specialized talents should take place. Supporters of this position tend to believe that schools should not offer intensive work in any area but only present a variety of areas for exploration and study. In English, for example, the gifted writer and the gifted mathematician alike would be exposed to a broad program of language and literature and have opportunities to use language and enjoy literature both for creative expression and for technical communication. Proponents of this view might agree that the gifted writer and the gifted mathematician should have opportunities for pursuing more intensive study of creative writing and of advanced mathematics but not at the expense of the individual's general education. Some supporters of this view argue that concentration of study in a single field at the secondary school level, though it may appeal to the talented individual, would perpetuate the existence of too many highly specialized persons who are essentially "ignorant" outside their own areas of talent. The general education proponents basically believe that the task of elementary and secondary schools is to lay the foundation for broad intellectual and creative interests, wide experience in the critical handling of ideas, skill in manipulation of basic problem solving, and a self-disciplined approach to learning. Specialization can and will then come readily at the tertiary level.

Another approach, conceptually opposite from the general educationist approach, argues that the elementary and secondary school years are of critical importance in the ultimate development of individual talents and gifts and that specialization should begin as early as feasible. Although agreeing that a gifted student needs a broad general education, they argue that acquiring such experiences should not preclude the opportunities to study intensively in an area in which a gifted individual has a particular aptitude, interest, and potential. Proponents of this position believe that the gifted student can acquire an appropriate general education and still specialize—the two are not antithetical but are, indeed, essential. The talented young mathematician who can learn the required mathematics of the general curriculum in a fraction of the usual time should then use the time saved, not for literature or art appreciation or study of a foreign language, but for more advanced courses in mathematics or for carrying out more advanced independent studies in an area of individual interest. The student with outstanding linguistic ability would not be compelled to study science or mathematics beyond the very basic requirements but would pursue development in his or her area of special aptitude. The outstanding musician would not give up advanced music studies in order to fulfill a requirement in mathematics or a foreign language. Supporters of this view believe that decreasing time available for intensive study in the area of the gifted student's talent by making other curricular demands actually penalizes the individual. Gifted students may resent inroads on their time resulting from requirements in curricular areas in which they have little interest and may, as a consequence, do only the minimum amount of work needed to get by. Thus, the goal of a broad background is not attained nor is the full development of the special talents.

The basic question is not whether there should be a broad general education at the expense of the development of specialized talents or vice versa but rather how both goals can be achieved through a balance. To achieve such a balance requires a clear conception of what constitutes a sound and appropriate general education—a broad liberal education that can serve as a basis for the development of specialized talents. It also requires a clear concept of how such an education can be achieved through appropriate and judicious acceleration so that there is sufficient time for specialized pursuits. Furthermore, it requires an understanding of what is an acceptable standard of achievement in general education areas.

A related issue of curricular balance is that of acceleration vis-à-vis enrichment—when and how to accelerate and when and how to enrich. This issue is often misstated as a question of acceleration versus enrichment. Acceleration, the provision of educational experinces at an earlier age or in less time than is normal, results in enrichment. At the simplest level, acceleration enables the student to deal with more advanced concepts at higher cognitive levels and thus represents an enriching experience. At another level, acceleration in one area provides opportunities for more advanced study in that area or for experiences in another area or areas. Enrichment involves breadth and/or depth—learning experiences that enable the student to probe more broadly or more intensively. It uses advanced resources aimed at enabling gifted individuals to attain higher levels of insight, understanding, performance, or product development. Both enrichment and acceleration have qualitative as well as quantitative dimensions; both enable the individual to pursue differential experiences through a greater variety of opportunities and engagements.

Given this view of acceleration and enrichment as alternative yet complementary approaches to learning opportunities for the gifted, the question becomes one of *when* it is more appropriate to alter the tempo or pace of instruction and *when* it is more appropriate to alter the breadth or depth of experience. Some experiences require time for the incubation of ideas, for reflection, for "playing around" with knowledge and ideas, for pursuit in depth employing a wide range of resources if they are to result in optimal learning. Some experiences focus on the acquisition of knowledge and skills, which, once mastered, are the basis for further learning. Some disciplines lend themselves to acceleration because gifted youngsters can acquire or master the knowledge and skills rapidly. Other learning must mature, and rapid acquisition is not sufficient by itself. Some disciplines, such as mathematics and foreign languages, lend themselves to acceleration, whereas other disciplines, such as literature or history, lend themselves to study in depth and breadth as well as creative reflection. Although gifted students are usually thought of as "rapid learners," acceleration is not always appropriate for talent development.

Another issue in curriculum development for the gifted is that of balance between cognitive and affective development. Most of the focus on curriculum development attends to cognitive development, to stimulation of problem-solving skills and other aspects of "thinking" and academic growth. Far less attention is given to the affect development of the gifted—feelings, values, interests, motivation, attitudes, morality, and self-concepts. There are studies of self-concepts and emotional problems of gifted children, for example, but these are quite different from teaching and learning in areas of the affective domain comparable to instruction in the cognitive domain. One can study a scientific problem intensely for its moral and value aspects as well as for its concepts and ideas. The importance of developing an idealism and social sensitivity among gifted persons requires that curricular attention be given to a balance between the cognitive and affective goals and interrelationships.

Moreover, pupils learn affective elements of growth from each other and from the climate in which they find themselves—elements such as self-concepts, attitudes toward more- and less-endowed peers, willingness to be "different," task commitment, motivation, acceptance of specific kinds of talents and talent areas, and willingness to participate in the school's system of rewards and punishment. The pursuit of excellence along many dimensions is determined by the affective climate. Behavioral nuances on the part of teachers, parents, adults, and fellow students affect student perceptions of the gifted. Psychological and emotional problems may or may not emerge as a consequence of special programs for the gifted. The climate of the classroom and the school, the interpersonal relationships therein, the structured and unstructured learning environments, and the formal and informal transactions are powerful mediators of both cognitive and affective growth.

There are important interactions between the formal and the informal curriculum, the planned and the subliminal curriculum. The climate created for the pursuit of excellence determines how committed individuals will be to participating in, grasping, or designing learning opportunities. Formal counseling and instruction may emerge from needs uncovered in the affective domain—for example, values orientation, personal guidance, ethics, and leadership training.

Another curricular issue focuses on the balance between individual and group activity in programs for the gifted. Independent study and individualized instruction are advocated for gifted students— opportunities to pursue their own interests, concerns, and problems on their own and by themselves. Although independent study is absolutely necessary for the development of the potential of the gifted individual, perhaps a more important consideration is the stimulation that comes from the interaction among gifted students. Sharing and communicating one's investigations or products with others is an important element of learning. Critiquing and evaluating the products and performances of one another is best done in group settings. Certain social learnings are optimally acquired in group settings. Although citizenship skills and knowledge may be acquired conceptually through independent study, citizenship is basically a social experience that can only be acquired through social intercourse. On the other hand, certain learning experiences require intensive and prolonged independent activity. A differentiated curriculum for the gifted must provide for both kinds of learning activities—group and individual—as is appropriate for the objectives being pursued.

Related to the questions about independent and group activities is the issue of balance regarding the grouping of gifted students. The issue of special groups, classes, or schools for the gifted has always been one of considerable controversy, and the arguments pro and con are well rehearsed in the literature. There has long been a recognition that the question of "homogeneous vs. heterogeneous grouping" is really the wrong question, although that debate continues. The issue is not whether gifted children should be isolated in completely self-contained settings or instructed in settings with children of diverse abilities and backgrounds. There are positive outcomes that come from the stimulation resulting from the interaction of gifted with other gifted and the competitiveness and cooperation that occurs, but there are other kinds of learnings that come from the interactions of the gifted with other children. For example, there is an understanding of diversity in any society and of the contributions that each individual is capable of making to a group's goals. The gifted student's affective development is especially influenced by the kind and quality of experiences he or she has with other individuals who are more or less gifted or who have different talents and gifts. A balance needs to be attained between learning experiences that are best engaged in with intellectual and creative peers and those that can only be experienced with other kinds of learners.

The question is essentially one of what kinds of groupings will facilitate particular kinds of appropriate learnings, both cognitive and affective. The end goal is one of nurturing individual potential while orienting the individual to society's needs for persons sensitive to the interdependence of humankind.

Issues also exist concerning a balance between internal, self-set standards of excellence and outstanding performance and externally determined standards. Gifted students are often much tougher in terms of the standards by which they judge their own products and performance than are the standards set by the school or by society at large. Most often, the school's judgment is based on test scores or teacher grades, usually more quantitative than qualitative. The gifted child may critique his or her own work on totally different qualitative dimensions. Test scores and teacher grades are significant factors in school and society's reward systems, yet they have severe shortcomings and limitations. The question educators of the gifted face is how to develop high standards of excellence and ways of judging excellence while meeting the demands of the system for high scores and grades, even when the two are not synchronized.

Still another issue concerns the allocation of time by gifted students. How much time should be allocated to the pursuit of one's interests when these differ from society's interests? For example, should the gifted student spend additional time in the laboratory, in the library, or in pursuit of his or her own interest—or should he or she become involved in some kind of community service activity? Should the gifted child work on an individual project rather than participate in some kind of team effort? Should the talented student mathematician devote time to an individual project for a Talent Search Contest or allocate scarce time resources to a team effort for the Mathematics Olympiad or the Olympics of the Mind?

Some argue that gifted children should allocate their time as they wish and that there is no particular obligation to divert time to service activities. Some even believe that by diverting their time, gifted children actually endanger the full development of their potential. Still others believe that the nature of the special talent determines how time devoted to it should be allocated. For instance, a precocious young musician may need to practice for long periods of time daily at an early age, whereas a gifted young scientist may have sufficient time for study available during the school day. Clearly, time allocation represents an issue in planning and counseling gifted students.

Finally, curricular questions arise regarding the education of the gifted in nonschool educative settings. Many agencies and institutions educate and socialize, and the cognitive and affective growth of gifted students are affected by the formal and structured as well as the informal and unstructured learning opportunities provided by the nonschool curriculums. The way in which giftedness is perceived and treated in the home and community, for example, has a significant impact on the affective development of the gifted. The family and community's values affect which talents will be valued and supported.

In addition, many personnel and material resources in the community's nonschool educative agencies can be used to enrich, challenge, and thus differentiate programs and services for the gifted. Community-centered experience-based learning extends the base for learning and makes the whole community a learning environment. In some instances gifted and talented students are so advanced in their areas of specialization that school-based resources are more limiting than enriching. By extending the learning environment into the community, educators can enrich the curriculum by making available human and material resources in a variety of agencies and settings. Mentor arrangements represent one avenue for nonschool programs for the gifted.

In Conclusion

A number of issues have been raised concerning differentiated curriculum and instruction. Although some biases may be inferred from the discussion of the issues, in fact there are no clear-cut, uniform, widely accepted resolutions. How curriculum planners resolve what are real and perennial issues depends on a variety of factors, including the basic philosophy concerning the nature and needs of the gifted and talented, the basic philosophy of education, the nature and number of gifted students being planned for, the human and material resources available in the school and community, the legal constraints, and so forth. Thus, no single formula is available to resolve these issues—it all depends!

In his study titled, "Concerning the Nature and Nurture of Genius," Pressey (1955) observed: "At any age, development of any ability is fostered by a favorable immediate environment, expert instruction, frequent and progressive opportunities for the exercise of the ability, social facilitation and frequent success experiences" (p. 125). These factors, which contributed to the nurture of gifted musicians and athletes whom Pressey studied, are equally applicable to the intellectual development of the gifted generally.

There are many valid and valuable "programs for the gifted" found in schools and communities across the country and in nations around the world. These involve various kinds of modifications and adaptations, instructional and administrative, aimed at providing "differentiated educational programs and/or services beyond those normally provided by the regular school program." However, a large and rich body of literature dealing with research and practice of nurturing the gifted suggests that an adequate and appropriate curriculum for the gifted encompasses the total learning environment, both school and nonschool, and not just that piece of the program usually labeled "gifted education." The intellectual, cognitive, and affective development of the gifted requires early identification, continuing nurturing, and, above all, consideration and resolution of the many curricular issues involved in such programs.

References

Clark, Barbara. *Growing Up Gifted.* Columbus: Charles E. Merrill Publishing Company, 1979.

Dishart, Martin. "Book Review: *The Gifted and the Talented—Their Education and Development." Educational Research* 9, 5 (March 1980): 22-26.

Guilford, J. P. "Three Faces of Intellect." *American Psychologist* 14 (1959): 469-479.

Guilford, J. P. *The Nature of Human Intelligence.* New York: McGraw-Hill Book Company, 1967.

Feldman, David Henry. "A Developmental Framework for Research with Gifted Children." In *Developmental Approaches to Giftedness and Creativity.* Edited by David Henry Feldman. San Francisco: Jossey-Bass Inc., 1982.

Marland, Sidney P., Jr. *Education of the Gifted and Talented.* Washington, D.C.: U.S. Government Printing Office, 1971.

Newland, T. Ernest. "The Gifted." *Review of Educational Research* XXIII (1955): 417-431.

Passow, A. Harry. "Differentiated Curricula for the Gifted/Talented: A Point of View." In *Curriculum for the Gifted,* pp. 4-20. Edited by Sandra N. Kaplan and others. Ventura, Calif.: Ventura County Superintendent of Schools Office, 1982.

Pressey, Sidney L. "Concerning the Nature and Nurture of Genius." *Scientific Monthly* 81(1955): 123-129.

Read, Peter B., "Foreword." In *Developmental Approaches to Giftedness and Creativity,* pp. 1-3. Edited by David Henry Feldman. San Francisco: Jossey-Bass Inc., 1982.

Renzulli, Joseph S. "What Makes Giftedness? Reexamining a Definition." *Phi Delta Kappan* 60 (November 1978): 180-184, 261.

Renzulli, Joseph S. "What We Don't Know about Programming for the Gifted and Talented." *Phi Delta Kappan* 61 (May 1980): 601-602.

Robinson, Halbert B. "Current Myths Concerning Gifted Children," *Gifted and Talented Brief No. 5.* Ventura, Calif.: Ventura County Superintendent of Schools Office, 1977, pp. 1-11.

Tannenbaum, Abraham J. *Gifted Children: Psychological and Educational Perspectives.* New York: Macmillan Publishing Co., 1983.

Taylor, Calvin W., and Ellison, Robert E. "Moving Toward Working Models in Creativity: Utah Creativity Experiences and Insights." In *Perspectives in Creativity*, pp. 191-223. Edited by Irving A. Taylor and Jacob W. Getzels. Chicago: Aldine Publishing Co., 1975.

Thurstone, I. L. *Multiple Factor Analysis: A Development and Expansion of "The Vectors of the Mind."* Chicago: University of Chicago Press, 1947.

Torrance, E. Paul. "Predicting the Creativity of Elementary School Children (1958-80)—and the Teacher Who 'Made a Difference'." *Gifted Child Quarterly* 25(1981): 55-61.

Torrance, E. Paul. "Creativity Research in Education: Still Alive," In *Perspectives in Creativity*, pp. 278-296. Edited by Irving A. Taylor and Jacob W. Getzels. Chicago: Aldine Publishing Company, 1975.

Ward, Virgil S. *Education of the Gifted: An Axiomatic Approach*. Columbus: Charles E. Merrill Publishing Co., 1961.

3. Critical Thinking: Its Nature, Measurement, and Improvement

Robert J. Sternberg

MORE THAN A DECADE HAS PASSED SINCE JOHN F. KENNEDY ORDERED the invasion of the Bay of Pigs. The invasion was to become one of the great disasters in U.S. political and military history. The invasion did not, of course, succeed in the ultimate overthrow of Cuba's Fidel Castro. More interesting, there is a widespread consensus among students of the situation that the invasion never had a chance to succeed. The decision to invade, made largely by Ivy-League-educated men with some experience in political affairs, was from almost any point of view, a lapse in critical thinking.

What is critical thinking, and how can well-educated men and women show lapses in it that are serious enough to lead to fiascos

Author's note: The project reported on in this chapter was performed pursuant to a grant from the National Institute of Education (NIE), Department of Education. The opinions expressed here do not necessarily reflect the position or policy of the NIE, and no official endorsement by the NIE should be inferred.

The NIE grant was administered through the Wisconsin Center for Education Research, and I am grateful to the Center for supporting preparation of this chapter. I am also grateful to E. Jean Gubbins for her permission to reproduce her matrix of thinking skills as Figure 3.1. Requests for reprints should be sent to Robert J. Sternberg, Department of Psychology, Yale University, Box 11A Yale Station, New Haven, CT 06520.

such as the Bay of Pigs, the Watergate break in and coverup, and any of a number of other similar events in our country's history? The goal of this essay is to define critical thinking, to review alternative approaches to understanding it, to compare some alternative procedures for measuring it, and to discuss some alternative attempts to train it.

A Definition of Critical Thinking

Construed broadly, *critical thinking comprises the mental processes, strategies, and representations people use to solve problems, make decisions, and learn new concepts.* The particular elements of critical thinking that people use vary widely both in scope and in quality across persons, tasks, and situations. Hence, it is necessary to specify in some detail just what the elements of critical thinking are and how they vary across persons, tasks, and situations. Such a specification is the goal of the following section.

Theories of the Nature of Critical Thinking

In some fields of education, it is difficult to get educational theorists to agree about anything. The field of critical thinking is distinctive for the amount of consensus among theorists regarding its nature. This is not to say that the consensus is complete, or that alternative theories and approaches to theorizing are nonexistent. It is to say, however, that the agreements clearly outweigh the disagreements. A review of theories and approaches suggests that the major differences are in how broadly or narrowly the construct of critical thinking is viewed—in its boundaries rather than in what is viewed to be the core.

Three Traditions of Theorizing

The study of critical thinking is of particular interest because it joins three traditions of thought—the educational, the philosophical, and the psychological. Indeed, if there is a modern-day founder of the "critical thinking movement," it is almost certainly John Dewey, who was simultaneously an educator, a philosopher, and a psychologist.

The philosophical tradition. The concern of philosophers with the elements of critical thinking dates back to ancient times. If Dewey is the modern-day founder of the critical-thinking movement, then Plato and Aristotle are its ancient founders. In more recent times, philosophers such as Ennis (in press), Lipman (in press), and Paul (in press) have devoted their attention to understanding the bases of critical thinking.

Philosophers have focused their attention not so much on the requirements of critical thinking in the classroom but on the requirements of formal logical systems. The difference in emphasis is important for two reasons.

First, the requirements of formal logical systems do not necessarily correspond to the requirements or capabilities of children in classroom situations. Indeed, the two sets of requirements may be completely different. For example, "resolution logic" provides a powerful method for proving certain logical theorems, but probably no one (in their right mind!) would claim that children spontaneously use resolution logic, or even that many of them would spontaneously adopt it after anything but extensive training. Not all philosophers have been quick to recognize the difference between the laws of logic and the laws of thought. Indeed, Boole (1954) entitled his book on "Boolean logic" *The Laws of Thought*, despite the fact that there is no evidence at all that people spontaneously adopt these laws in their thought.

Second, it may perhaps be better to think of the requirements of logical systems as providing models of competence rather than models of performance for human thought. The rules of logic can tell us how people might think critically under ideal circumstances in which the limitations typically placed on the human information-processing system are not in place. But numerous potential limitations ordinarily block the use of our full competence—limited time, limited information, limited working memory capacity, limited motivation, and so on.

These two delimitations on the interpretation of philosophical theories are not criticisms of philosophical approaches. We need to know the maximum potentials of critical thought, lest we settle for less precision and less reflectivity in our thinking than that of which we are capable. At the same time, we need to recognize the personal and situational constraints that often impinge on our working up to full capacity.

The psychological tradition. Psychologists interested in the nature of critical thinking, such as Bransford and Stein (1984), Bruner (1960, 1961), Feuerstein (1980), and Sternberg (1985), have been particularly concerned with characterizing critical thinking as it is performed under the limitations of the person and the environment. For example, Feuerstein (1980) specified how the critical thinking of retarded performers differs from that of normal performers; Sternberg and Davidson (1983), in contrast, compared the critical thinking of gifted and normal performers. None of these theorists, though, has proposed a model of totally rational thinking. Indeed, Guyote and Sternberg's (1981) work is more typical of psychological theorizing in pinpointing how people differ from the fully rational performer in solving syllogisms.

Psychological theorizing can be valuable in showing how people think critically in the absence of full information, unlimited time, perfect memory, and so on. At the same time, two cautions must be observed in evaluating the theories of many psychologists.

First, the theories of psychologists are often derived from and tested on performance of human subjects in laboratory settings, and there is no guarantee that people will perform in their everyday lives (especially in the classroom) in the same ways that they do in the laboratory. To the contrary, most available evidence suggests consequential differences in the two kinds of settings of performance.

Second, the constraints of proposing theories that are empirically testable through the standard means of psychological experimentation sometimes results in theories that oversimplify the analysis of critical thinking. The constraints of testability contributes to scientific analysis—but often at the expense of oversimplification.

The educational tradition. In the educational tradition of theorizing are leading figures such as Bloom (1956), Gagne (1980), Perkins (1981), and Renzulli (1976), whose theorizing seems directly responsive to the skills needed by children in the classroom for problem solving, decision making, and concept learning. Bloom's (1956) famous taxonomy of cognitive skills and Gagne's (1965) well-known hierarchy of learning skills have seen widespread application in classroom situations and even textbook creation. These theorists have drawn heavily on classroom observation, text analysis, and process analysis of thinking in the classroom to guide their thinking about critical thinking.

Educational theories have the advantage of being closely tied to classroom observation and experience. At the same time, two points should be kept in mind when using or evaluating these theories.

First, the educational theories often do not have the clarity in epistemological status characteristic of the philosophical and psychological theories, making it more difficult, in some respects, both to evaluate and to use the educational theories. Philosophical theories tend to be competence theories specifying what people can do; psychological theories tend to be performance theories specifying what people actually do; educational theories are often a mixture of the two, with the nature and proportions of the mix less than clearly specified. To this day, for example, educators argue over the extent to which Bloom's taxonomy represents a prescriptive versus a descriptive model of human thought.

Second, in my experience, educationally based theories tend not to have been subjected to tests of the same degree of rigor that has characterized the testing of philosophical and psychological theories. Philosophical theories based on various kinds of logics must be logically rigorous and internally consistent. Psychological theories based on human performance must be externally consistent with respect to the behavior they purport to describe. Educational theories are often not subjected either to the logical tests of philosophical theories or to the psychological tests of the psychological theories.

A Framework for Theories of the Nature of Critical Thinking

Because there are so many accounts of critical thinking, and because they so often say similar things in different ways (or even occasionally different things in similar ways), it becomes important to develop some kind of framework that can encompass the various theories and to highlight their similarities and differences.

The framework proposed here is based on that generated by my triarchic theory of human intelligence (Sternberg, 1985). The framework was derived in large part by classifying the goals and scope of many previous theories of intellectual functioning. In the present context, I propose that theories of critical thinking can, and often do, deal with one or more aspects of critical thinking—its relation to the mind of the individual, its relation to the context in which it occurs, and its relation to the experience of the individual with various kinds of tasks and situations previously confronted that required critical thinking in greater or lesser degree.

The Relation of Critical Thinking to the Internal World of the Individual. Theories of the internal workings of the mind when it engages in critical thinking can be seen as being aimed at the very essence of what critical thinking is about: What do we do when we think critically, and how do we do it?

Students of critical thinking have proposed various taxonomies of skills purported to span the range of critical thinking. Consider three examples of such taxonomies, one each from the philosophical, psychological, and educational traditions.

1. *A philosophical taxonomy: Ennis (in press).* Ennis, a philosopher, has suggested that critical thinking results from the interaction of a set of dispositions toward critical thinking with a set of abilities for critical thinking.

The dispositions include, among others, (a) seeking a clear statement of the thesis or question, (b) seeking reasons, (c) trying to be well informed, and (d) trying to remain relevant to the main point. The idea underlying the listing of dispositions is that a prerequisite for critical thinking is the motivation or desire to think critically.

Ennis classifies abilities under five main categories, which are themselves further subdivided. The categories are elementary clarification, basic support, inference, advanced clarification, and strategy and tactics.

Elementary clarification consists of focusing on a question, analyzing arguments, and asking and answering questions of clarification and/or challenge. Basic support involves judging the credibility of a source and observing and judging observation reports. Inference comprises deducing and judging deductions, inducing and judging inductions, and making and judging value judgments. Advanced clarification involves defining terms, judging definitions, and identifying assumptions. Finally, strategy and tactics include deciding on an action and interacting with others. These categories are all themselves further subdivided (see Ennis, in press).

2. *A psychological taxonomy: Sternberg (1985).* My own taxonomy derives not from a logical but from a psychological analysis of critical thinking. According to my own "componential" account of thought, the skills involved in critical thinking are of three kinds: metacomponents, performance components, and knowledge-acquisition components.

Metacomponents are higher order executive processes used to plan what one is going to do, monitor is while one is doing it, and evaluate it after it is done. The metacomponents include recognizing that a problem exists, defining the nature of the problem, deciding on a set of steps for solving the problem, ordering these steps into a coherent strategy, deciding on a form a mental representation for information, allocating one's time and resources in solving a problem, monitoring one's solution to a problem as the problem is being solved, and using feedback regarding problem solving after one's problem solving has been completed. Similar taxonomies have been proposed by Brown (1978) and Bransford and Stein (1984).

Performance components are lower order, nonexecutive processes used to execute the instructions of the metacomponents and provide feedback to them. Performance components vary by domain of performance, for example, inductive reasoning, deductive reasoning, spatial visualization, reading, and so on. Consider, for example, the performance components of induction. These include encoding stimuli, comparing stimuli, inferring relations between stimuli, mapping relations between relations, applying relations from one domain to another, justifying potential responses, and responding.

Knowledge-acquisition components are the processes used to learn concepts or procedures. Three such components are selective encoding, which involves screening relevant from irrelevant information; selective combination, which involves putting together the relevant information in a coherent and organized way; and selective comparison, which involves relating old, previously known information to new, about-to-be-learned information.

3. *An educational taxonomy: Bloom (1956).* Bloom has proposed a hierarchical taxonomy for cognitive information processing. At the lowest level is knowledge. The next level is comprehension, which requires one to go beyond knowledge in that one must understand what one comes to know. At the next level is application, which is a level higher yet in that the individual must also be able to apply what he or she has comprehended. A level higher up is analysis, which requires one to appraise critically what one comprehends and applies. Still higher is synthesis, which requires putting together in a somewhat creative way the knowledge one has analyzed in various domains. At the highest level is evaluation, which is a broad and critical appraisal of the knowledge one has analyzed and synthesized.

In this section, I have described three taxonomies of critical thinking skills. Although the organizations of these taxonomies are different, as are the exact thinking skills they comprise, the overlap among the taxonomies is striking. All of the theorists cited believe in the importance of learning, comprehension, deductive reasoning, and inductive reasoning skills. The names they give to the various skills within each of these domains differ, but the skills seem to differ hardly at all, except with respect to how finely differentiated and how broadly encompassing they are within one or another theory. Thus, it appears that there may be a certain core of critical thinking skills that would appear in any reasonably complete list. In fact, Joan Gubbins of the Connecticut State Department of Education has surveyed a large number of similar taxonomies and has developed a list that reflects the skills listed by numerous theorists. Figure 3.1 (p. 52) contains the various thinking skills in Gubbins' (1985) list.

The Relation of Critical Thinking to the Experience of the Individual. It is one thing to apply critical thinking to tasks and situations that are familiar to us but quite another to apply it to tasks and situations that are unfamiliar. Often the processes and strategies that come so easily to us in familiar situations simply resist implementation in strange tasks and situations. The processes and strategies may or may not be different in the novel task or situation. Sometimes it is

Figure 3.1. Gubbins' Matrix of Thinking Skills

I. Problem Solving

    A.   Identifying general problem
    B.   Clarifying problem
    C.   Formulating hypothesis
    D.   Formulating appropriate questions
    E.   Generating related ideas
    F.   Formulating alternative solutions
    G.   Choosing best solution
    H.   Applying the solution
    I.   Monitoring acceptance of the solution
    J.   Drawing conclusions

II. Decision Making

    A.   Stating desired goal/condition
    B.   Stating obstacles to goal/condition
    C.   Identifying alternatives
    D.   Examining alternatives
    E.   Ranking alternatives
    F.   Choosing best alternative
    G.   Evaluating actions

III. Inferences

    A.   Inductive thinking skills
        1.   Determining cause and effect
        2.   Analyzing open-ended problems
        3.   Reasoning by analogy
        4.   Making inferences
        5.   Determining relevant information
        6.   Recognizing relationships
        7.   Solving insight problems
    B.   Deductive thinking skills
        1.   Using logic
        2.   Spotting contradictory statements
        3.   Analyzing syllogisms
        4.   Solving spatial problems

IV. Divergent Thinking Skills

    A.   Listing attributes of objects/situation
    B.   Generating multiple ideas (fluency)
    C.   Generating different ideas (flexibility)
    D.   Generating unique ideas (originality)
    E.   Generating detailed ideas (elaboration)
    F.   Synthesizing information

V. Evaluative Thinking Skills

    A.   Distinguishing between facts and opinions
    B.   Judging credibility of a source
    C.   Observing and judging observation reports
    D.   Identifying central issues and problems
    E.   Recognizing underlying assumptions
    F.   Detecting bias, stereotypes, cliches
    G.   Recognizing loaded language
    H.   Evaluating hypotheses
    I.   Classifying data
    J.   Predicting consequences
    K.   Demonstrating sequential synthesis of information
    L.   Planning alternative strategies
    M.   Recognizing inconsistencies in information
    N.   Identifying stated and unstated reasons
    O.   Comparing similarities and differences
    P.   Evaluating arguments

VI. Philosophy and Reasoning

    A.   Using dialogical/dialectical approaches

This matrix is based on a compilation and distillation of ideas from Bloom, Bransford, Bruner, Carpenter, Dewey, Ennis, Feuerstein, Jones, Kurfman, Kurfman and Solomon, Lipman, Orlandi, Parnes, Paul, Perkins, Renzulli, Sternberg, Suchman, Taba, Torrance, Upton, the Ross Test, the Whimbey Analytical Skills Test, The Cornell Critical Thinking Test, the Cognitive Abilities Test, the Watson-Glaser Critical Thinking Appraisal, the New Jersey Test of Reasoning Skills, and the SEA Test.

their readiness for implementation that differs between familiar and unfamiliar situations. Again, consider three alternative but related views of the role of novel experience in critical thinking.

1. *A philosophical view: Paul (in press).* According to philosopher Richard Paul, an essential element of critical thinking—perhaps *the* essential element—is the ability to see things from others' points of view, which may be quite novel and even foreign with respect to one's point of view. Paul refers to such thinking as *dialogical.* For example, the ability of a liberal to see things from a conservative point of view, the ability of a husband to take his wife's point of view on the desirability of sharing housework, and the ability of an adult to see things through a child's eyes, are all examples of dialogical thinking. Such thinking is necessary to escape the egocentrism and narrowness of perspective that characterize the "unilogical" thinking in which most of us so often indulge.

2. *A psychological view: Sternberg (1985).* My own experiential account of critical thinking strongly emphasizes the importance of coping with novelty. There is good reason for this emphasis: It is often in the novel task or situation—such as the Bay of Pigs or the Watergate crisis mentioned earlier—that the potentials for either great gain or serious loss present themselves. Indeed, the great contributions to the world are often traceable to major insights in which an ingenious individual has seen a new and useful way to solve a problem, whether a new one or an old one.

According to Sternberg and Davidson (1983; see also Davidson & Sternberg, 1984), insight is an important part of the ability to deal with novelty. We propose that insights are of three kinds—selective encoding, selective combination, and selective comparison, as discussed earlier. Thus, the processes of insight do not differ from the process of knowledge acquisition in more ordinary critical thinking. What does differ, however, is the knowledge base to which these processes can be brought to bear. In ordinary thinking, we have a set of clues or guidelines or rules we can use to help us learn new things. In insightful thinking, we do not have such a readily available set of clues, guidelines, or rules. We must make up the rules as we go along, and it is in this sense that an insight is a leap into the unknown: it is a leap not only in knowledge but in the way in which that knowledge is acquired.

3. *An educational view: de Bono (1967, 1969).* de Bono has proposed a series of techniques for enhancing people's critical thinking. One of the most well-known of these is what he refers to as PMI: plus, minus, interesting. What, exactly, does this mean?

Consider a series of alternative solutions to a given problem; for example, what we would do if all money in the world instantly became worthless. (de Bono's interest in developing the ability of his readers and listeners to deal with novelty can be seen right away in his choice of problems, many of which are highly novel.) de Bono suggests that as each alternative solution to a complex problem is posed, one should list the positive (*plus*), negative (*minus*), and *interesting features of that solution. de Bono's view is unusual for its stress on the evaluation of the interest as well as the positive and negative features of each solution. Getting people to think in this way encourages them to develop their ability to see both familiar and unfamiliar problems in novel and potentially interesting ways.

Once again, underlying the differences in language, there appears to be a common core of beliefs regarding the nature of the ability to deal with novelty. Insights almost inevitably involve some degree of dialogical thinking. They require us to perceive a problem we may have been pondering for quite some time from a new and different perspective. Most of the classical insight problems, such as the "nine-dot" problem, require us to see a given problem from a new and seemingly unusual vantage point. In the nine-dot problem, for example, one must connect nine dots arranged in a 3×3 matrix with no more than four pencil lines, without ever lifting one's pencil from the paper. Solution of the problem requires one to recognize that one must go outside the implicit perimeter defined by the dots in order to be able to connect them. Similarly, truly insightful thoughts are generally interesting thoughts, even if the insights turn out to be wrong. Indeed, encouraging people to think in "interesting" ways may be tantamount to encouraging them to think more insightfully. Thus, whatever the language the various theorists use, their conception of the role of novelty in critical thinking seems to be highly similar, although certainly not identical.

The relation of critical thinking to the external world of the individual. Perhaps the single question that most directly motivates this section is: critical thinking for what? If innumerable studies of transfer of training have revealed anything, it is that transfer is exceedingly difficult to attain. Teaching thinking skills or any other skills in any one context does not assure, or even render likely, their transfer to another context. Moreover, it is not even immediately obvious that critical thinking skills are the same in all situations. Certainly, their instantiations differ. Critical thinking skills should be taught in a way that maximizes the probability of their transfer to real-life situations. Different theorists have recognized this necessity in different ways.

1. *A philosophical approach: Lipman (1974).* Lipman's program for training thinking skills, Philosophy for Children, presents these skills in the context of the everyday lives of children (see Lipman and Sharp, 1975; Lipman, Sharp, and Oscanyan, 1977). The basic format of the program has students reading novels about children in their everyday worlds and about how those children bring critical thinking to bear on their worlds. Students are not left to figure out how to bridge the gap between critical thinking skills and everyday life. Rather, in all phases of the program, they are provided with explicit models of how this bridging can be done.

2. *Two psychological approaches: Bransford and Stein (1984) and Sternberg (1985).* Bransford and Stein's book on the "ideal" problem solver, demonstrates almost all of the techniques presented through everyday examples. The techniques for problem solving are "brought to life" through concrete instances, and readers are encouraged immediately to apply the techniques to problems they face in their own lives.

Sternberg (1985) takes a somewhat different approach, initially illustrating methods of critical thinking through concrete examples but then providing exercises that range from the academic to the practical. The idea motivating this variation in types of context is that students will best learn how to apply processes and strategies of critical thinking in their everyday lives if they use these processes and strategies in the broadest possible array of circumstances, ranging from the most academic to the most practical.

Both Bransford and Stein's and Sternberg's approaches contrast with the approach of Feuerstein (1980), in which problems (or "instruments," as Feuerstein calls them) are largely academic and abstract in nature. Feuerstein calls for bridging of cognitive skills to students' everyday lives, but this bridging is pretty much left to the teacher. Thus, it is less controlled in terms of how and how much it occurs. From the present point of view, this deemphasis on the external world of the individual in the training would tend to have less favorable implications for transfer than would the greater emphasis of other programs.

3. *An educational approach: Head Start.* Perhaps the best example of educational philosophy for bridging the gap between thinking skills and the real world was embodied in the numerous Head Start programs of the 1960s, some of which continue in modified form to the present day. There was no one consistent philosophy or even psychological theory behind these programs. Many programs seem to have had no particular philosophical or theoretical underpinnings at all.

What the programs did have was a commitment on the part of their initiators to making a difference in children's lives, particularly in their schooling. However one evaluates the outcomes of these programs, one would have to give them credit for making educators and laypeople realize that intellectual skills are potentially trainable. These programs were transitional between nothing, on the one hand, and the theory-based programs of today, on the other.

Tests for Measuring Critical Thinking

Several tests have been advanced that purport to measure critical-thinking skills. The tests overlap to a large degree in the skills they measure. Nevertheless, some differences are worthy of note. The purpose of this section is not to provide an exhaustive review of all of the available tests but rather to illustrate some of the basic principles underlying these tests and to show how these principles relate across the range of tests available. The emphasis will be on tests at the secondary-school level.

1. *Three philosophically derived tests: The Watson-Glaser Critical Thinking Appraisal, the Cornell Critical Thinking Test, and the New Jersey Test of Reasoning Skills.* All three of these tests are derived from the philosophical tradition of measuring critical thinking. They are highly overlapping conceptually.

The Watson-Glaser Critical Thinking Appraisal (Watson & Glaser, 1980) contains five subtests, each measuring a somewhat different critical thinking skill. There are two forms of the test, each containing a total of 80 items. Untimed administration is recommended, although an optimal time limit of 40 minutes can be imposed (in which case subtest scores will be less interpretable, as timing is for the test as a whole, and subjects may not complete later subtests). The test is suitable for individuals at the Grade 9 level and above.

The five subtests are (a) Inference, which requires discrimination among degrees of validity of inferences drawn from given data; (b) Recognition of Assumptions, which requires recognition of assertions; (c) Deduction, which requires determination of given statements of premises; (d) Interpretation, which involves weighing of evidence and deciding if generalizations or conclusions based on the given data are warranted; and (e) Evaluation of Arguments, which requires distinguishing between arguments that are strong and relevant and those that are weak or irrelevant to a particular question at issue. The actual test items have high face validity, in that they draw on classroom and general life situations.

Various norms are available, including high school norms (by grade), norms for various college and university groups, and various occupational norms. The main kind of score is the percentile equivalent to a given raw score. Split-half reliability coefficients for various groups generally range in the .70s for the test as a whole. Correlations with intelligence tests are variable but seem to center at about the .6 level with verbally weighted tests. It is not clear whether the test has incremental validity in predicting various kinds of performances beyond that which would be obtained with a student-group intelligence test.

The Cornell Critical Thinking Test (Ennis and Millman, 1971) is based on Ennis's conception of critical thinking, as briefly described earlier. The test is available in two levels, X and Z. Level X is appropriate for secondary school (Grade 7) and beyond, Level Z primarily for college students (and bright secondary-school students). Level X has 71 questions and a time limit of 50 minutes. Level Z has 52 questions but the same time limit as Level X.

Level X contains four sections. The first section contains items asking for the bearing, if any, of information on a hypothesis. The hypothesis is in every case a general statement. Examinees must indicate whether a particular hypothesis is warranted by the data. The second section is concerned with measuring examinees' ability to judge the reliability of information on the basis of its source and the conditions under which it is obtained. The third section measures students' ability to judge whether a statement follows from its premises, and the fourth section involves identification of assumptions.

Level Z contains seven sections, measuring the examinees's ability to (a) indicate whether a statement follows from its premises, (b) detect equivocal arguments, (c) evaluate reliability of observations and authenticity of sources, (d) judge the direction of support, if any, for a given hypothesis, (e) focus on choosing of useful predictions for hypothesis testing, (f) define terms, and (g) spot gaps in arguments.

Norms for both levels of the Cornell Critical Thinking Test are given as percentile equivalents. Internal consistency reliabilities for various groups appear to center around .8 for Level X and around .7 for Level Z. Correlations with other tests are variable. They seem to center around .5 for verbally oriented intelligence tests. The reported correlation with the Watson-Glaser, .48, is no higher than the correlation of the test with verbal IQ and scholastic aptitude measures. The correlation of the Cornell with the ACE Test of Critical Thinking, .44, is also no better than the correlation of the Cornell with the Watson-Glaser. These data are not auspicious in indicating a clear, differentiable construct of "critical thinking" apart from general verbal intelligence.

The third of the philosophically based tests to be described here is the New Jersey test of Reasoning Skills, Form B, developed by Virginia Shipman (1983) of the Educational Testing Service and promoted in conjunction with Lipman's Philosophy for Children program. The New Jersey Test of Reasoning Skills is a 50-item inventory purporting to measure 22 different skill areas: converting statements, translating into logical form, inclusion/exclusion, recognizing improper questions, avoiding jumping to conclusions, analogical reasoning, detecting underlying assumptions, eliminating alternatives, inductive reasoning, reasoning with relationships, detecting ambiguities, discerning causal relationships, identifying good reasons, recognizing symmetrical relationships, categorical syllogistic reasoning, distinguishing differences of kind and degree, recognizing transitive relationships, recognizing dubious authority, reasoning with four-possibilities matrices, contradicting statements, whole–part and part–whole reasoning, and conditional syllogistic reasoning. Like the other tests, this one is highly verbal. Its reliabilities are reported to be in the mid to high .80s, and it is reported to correlate at the .6 to .8 level with subtests of the New Jersey College Basic Skills Placement Test, which is a test of verbal and mathematical skills emphasizing achievement at least as much as aptitude. The fact that the New Jersey Test of Reasoning Skills correlates at the .8 level with the "Reading Comprehension" and "Sentence Sense" subtests of the placement test might be seen by some as slightly disturbing: all three of the tests described so far are highly verbally loaded, and one might well wonder as to the extent that what they measure is separable from general verbal skills. Indeed, the little evidence accumulated so far does not indicate a clear separation at all, perhaps because a fairly high level of verbal comprehension is prerequisite for high scores on all of these tests.

2. *A psychologically derived test: The Triarchic Test of Intellectual Skills.* This test is new, is currently available in two forms only from the author (Sternberg), and is not yet normed. The triarchic test is based on Sternberg's (1985) triarchic theory of intelligence and, hence, does not purport to separate critical thinking from intelligence. The test is appropriate for high school and college levels. The 12 untimed subtests of the triarchic test are equally divided between verbal and nonverbal content and measure (a) metacomponential thinking skills (planning, monitoring, evaluating), (b) performance-componential skills (inferring relations, applying relations, mapping higher order

relations between domains), (c) knowledge-acquisition componential skills (learning concepts in natural contexts), (d) ability to deal with novelty (distinguishing relevant from irrelevant information, combining relevant information in a logical way, bringing previously acquired knowledge to bear on the acquisition and understanding of new knowledge), (e) automatization of information processing (making conscious and controlled processing subconscious and automatized), and (f) adaptive flexibility (bringing the various kinds of skills described above to bear on everyday adaptation, as in route planning and evaluating inferential fallacies in everyday reasoning). No normative, reliability, or validity information are yet available.

To conclude, several tests are available for measuring critical thinking skills. The philosophically based ones are highly loaded verbally but measure reasoning in the verbal context rather than straight knowledge or fact comprehension. The distinguishability of their scores from verbal intelligence is marginal. The psychologically based test contains both verbal and nonverbal test items. This test makes no attempt to distinguish between critical thinking and intellectual skills. All of the tests provide means for assessing reasoning without heavy demands upon students' knowledge base.

Programs for Training Critical Thinking

Programs for training critical thinking skills have been with us for thousands of years, although they have not always been recognized as such. The traditional name for such programs has been "logic," and at the college level such courses have usually been taught in philosophy departments. A complete review of programs for training critical thinking skills would obviously be beyond the bounds of this article (but see Nickerson, Perkins, and Smith, in press; Wagner and Sternberg, 1984). Nevertheless, it is possible to say something about the range of such programs. The emphasis here will again be at the secondary level.

2. *A philosophically based program: Copi (1978).* At the secondary–college level, courses in logic have traditionally developed students' critical thinking skills. Texts on logic remain among the best of the philosophically based programs for secondary and college students. One of the most well-known such texts is Copi (1978), which has gone through five editions.

Copi's course consists of three basic parts: use of language in logic, deduction, and induction. The part on language in turn consists of four chapters: (1) an opening, introductory chapter on the nature of logic, (2) uses of language in logical thinking, (3) informal fallacies, and (4) definition. The part on deduction consists of six chapters: (5) categorical propositions (e.g., the nature of "all" and "some" statements and the use of affirmation and negation in logic), (6) categorical syllogisms (i.e., combination of categorical statements into full-fledged logical reasoning problems, such as "All men are mortals. Some mortals are human. Can one be assured that all men are human?"), (7) arguments in ordinary language, (8) symbolic logic (i.e., deductive reasoning when symbols rather than ordinary-language statements are used as premises and conclusions), (9) methods of deduction, and (10) quantification theory (i.e., full-fledged logical proof). The part on induction consists of four chapters: (11) analogy and probable inference, (12) causal arguments, (13) philosophy of science and hypothesis testing, and (14) probability theory.

Copi's course is fairly typical of logic texts as vehicles for teaching critical thinking. There is really no substitute for logic courses, in that none of the other kinds of courses provide the full power of the philosophical discipline for the understanding and analysis of logical arguments. At the same time, logic courses do not provide full training in critical thinking. For one thing, they tend to deal only with problems and situations where the methods of logic directly apply. Yet any problem solver quickly learns that many of life's problems do not lend themselves to formal logical analysis. In addition, the problems they present tend to be much more structural than many of the problems people typically encounter. Moreover, logic courses fail fully to take into account the performance limitations on human competence (e.g., memory capacity or time or priorities for problem solving). Psychologically based courses on critical thinking try to go beyond straightforward logic courses to deal with some of these problems.

2. *Psychologically based programs: Bransford and Stein (1984) and Sternberg (1986).* Many programs based on psychological theories or principles have been proposed. Two of the most recent such courses are those of Bransford and Stein (1984) and of Sternberg (1986).

Bransford and Stein's course is called *The Ideal Problem Solver,* where *IDEAL* is an acronym for five steps in what Bransford and Stein seem to perceive as ideal problem solving: *I*dentifying the problem, *D*efining and representing the problem, *E*xploring possible strategies, *A*cting on the strategies, *L*ooking back and evaluating the effects of one's activities.

The course is presented in a brief (150-page) paperback book containing eight chapters, plus appendices, answers to exercises, and indices. The chapters cover (1) the importance of problem solving, (2) the model for improving problem solving, (3) improving memory skills, (4) learning with understanding, (5) intelligent criticism, (6) creativity, (7) effective communication, and (8) concluding remarks. The program is impressive for its lucidity, breadth, brevity, effective use of concrete examples, and connection to psychological theory and research. If the course has a weakness, it is perhaps in the limited coverage possible in a very brief text. This is a weakness only if one is seeking an in-depth course in critical thinking rather than a concise guide, which the *IDEAL* book certainly provides.

Sternberg's (1986) *Understanding and Increasing Intelligence* draws even more heavily on psychological theory than does the *IDEAL* program. In the case of Sternberg's program, the theory is his own triarchic theory of human intelligence (Sternberg, 1985). The organization of the book and teachers' guide are shown in Figure 3.2. This program is larger in scope than is Bransford and Stein's. It is intended to serve as a year-long, or minimally, semester-long course. Moreover, whereas the *IDEAL* course is designed primarily for individual reading by individual people, the Sternberg course is designed such that reading of the text (which can stand on its own) is ideally supplemented by class discussion, papers, supplementary activities, and the like.

Sternberg's program is based upon several key instructional principles. First, one must teach for transfer, rather than by merely hoping it will occur. The program does so by including problems that range from academic to practical, that range widely in content (that is, mathematics, logic, reading, science, social studies), that range from familiar to unfamiliar, and that range from abstract to quite concrete. The idea is to instantiate the basic processes of the triarchic theory in as broad a range of problem types as possible.

Second, the program emphasizes motivating both students and teachers. A key motivational device is teaching the students and teachers about the theory and how it serves as a useful basis for a program to train intellectual skills.

Third, the program emphasizes training of metacomponents (executive processes) as well as performance components and knowledge-acquisition components (nonexecutive processes), as well as their application to novel and real-world situations. Thus, the instruction covers the full range of stipulations of the underlying psychological theory.

Finally, the program has an entire chapter on emotional and motivational blocks to the use of one's intelligence. These blocks include dispositions such as fear of failure, lack of follow through, task-com-

---

Figure 3.2. Organization of *Understanding and Increasing Your Intelligence: A Triarchic Program for Training Intellectual Skills* (Sternberg, 1986)

STUDENTS' TEXT

Part I. Background
    Chapter 1: Some Historical Background on Views of Intelligence and Attempts
           to Increase It
    Chapter 2: The Triarchic Theory of Human Intelligence

Part II. The Internal World of the Individual: Components of Human Intelligence
    Chapter 3: Metacomponents (executive processes used to plan, monitor, and evaluate
           problem-solving performance)
    Chapter 4: Performance Components (nonexecutive processes used to execute the instruc-
           tions of metacomponents)
    Chapter 5: Knowledge-Acquisition Components (nonexecutive processes used to learn
           how to solve problems)

Part III. The Experience of the Individual: Facts of Human Intelligence
    Chapter 6: Coping with Novelty
    Chapter 7: Automatizing Information Processing

Part IV. The External World of the Individual: Functions of Human Intelligence
    Chapter 8: Practical Intelligence

Part V. Personality, Motivation, and Intelligence
    Chapter 9: Why Intelligent People Fail (Too Often)

INSTRUCTOR'S MANUAL

1. Purpose of Chapter
2. Chapter Outline
3. Main Ideas
4. Questions for Class Discussion
5. Suggested Paper Topics
6. Supplementary Activities
7. Suggested Readings
8. Suggested Time Allocation

---

pletion difficulties, misattribution of blame for failure, and the like. The goal of this chapter is to make students aware of the impediments that often prevent them from making the most of whatever intellectual skills they have.

    3. *An educationally based program: Whimbey and Lochhead (1982). Problem Solving and Comprehension* (third edition). A course at the high school–college level prepared by Arthur Whimbey and Jack Lochhead, Problem Solving and Comprehension is fairly typical of educationally based programs for training critical thinking skills. It can be used as a main text or as a supplementary text on courses on critical

thinking. The book contains 11 chapters on the following topics, plus appendices: (1) test your mind, (2) errors in reasoning, (3) problem-solving methods, (4) verbal reasoning problems, (5) six myths about reading, (6) analogies, (7) writing relationship sentences, (8) how to form analogies, (9) analysis of trends and patterns, (10) solving mathematical word problems, and (11) the "post-wasi test." There is no particular psychological theory underlying the program, and the order of the chapters seems to be somewhat arbitrary. Problems tend to be fairly academic, and no specific provisions appear to be built into the program to encourage transfer. Primarily, what students get is a lot of practice in problem solving and fairly minimal instruction in general techniques of problem solving. The course does not contain the fairly elaborate motivational aids of the two courses discussed above, nor does it contain many real-world problems.

Conclusions

I have presented in this chapter a brief overview of some of the main issues in the study of critical thinking: its nature, its measurement, and its improvement. Although there is still a long way to go, we have come remarkably far during the last few years in advancing our understanding of critical thinking. We have some good ideas both about how to test it and how to train it. At the same time, we need to recognize some of the limitations of our present understanding.

First, we have a much better understanding of analytical (critical) thinking than we do of synthetic (creative) thinking. This imbalance in our understanding is not for a lack of attempts to understand creative thinking (e.g., Amabile, 1983; Perkins, 1981). Rather, creative thinking seems to be much more resistant to analysis. Yet the most important contributions of thinking to the world and its cultures are probably in the synthetic domain rather than in the analytic one.

Second, existing tests seem only to scratch the surface of critical thinking, and to do that even in flawed ways. We have seen how many existing tests tend to be highly "verbally loaded." Indeed, what these tests measure is not clearly distinguishable from verbal intelligence as it is traditionally operationalized in standard tests of intelligence. Moreover, there is a large gap between the ability to apply critical thinking in fairly trivial, highly structured, and usually multiple-choice tests, on the one hand, and in one's everyday life, on the other. None of the tests came even close to bridging this gap.

Third, our training programs for improving critical thinking are themselves in need of improvement (see Sternberg, in press, for a critique of these programs). The programs, like the tests, do not fully bridge the gap between the classroom situation and situations outside it. Moreover, with few exceptions, the programs tend to be fairly narrow both in the range of skills they cover and in the instantiations within which these skills are instantiated.

The current concern of educators with critical thinking offers students a new chance for developing critical thinking skills. This chance will come to naught, however, if the concern proves to be nothing more than a brief infatuation, if training in critical thinking is not brought into all aspects of classroom endeavor, or if the concern stays only a concern and is not followed through with large-scale interventions. Training in critical thinking should not be the privilege of a selected intellectual minority or the luxury of the upper class. It should be the right of every student, and it is our responsibility to all our students to enable them to exercise this right.

References

Amabile, T.M. *The Social Psychology of Creativity.* New York: Springer Press, 1983.

Bloom, B.S., ed. *Taxonomy of Educational Objectives: The Classification of Educational Goals. Handbook I: Cognitive Domain.* New York: David McKay, 1956.

Boole, G. *The Investigation of the Laws of Thought.* London: Walton & Maberly, 1954.

Bransford, J.D., and Stein, B.S. *The Ideal Problem Solver: A Guide for Improving Thinking, Learning and Creativity.* San Francisco: Freeman, 1984.

Brown, A.L. "Knowing When, Where, and How to Remember: A Problem of Metacognition." In *Advances in Instructional Psychology (Vol. 1).* Edited by R. Glaser. Hillsdale, N.J.: Erlbaum, 1978.

Bruner, J.S. *The Process of Education.* Cambridge: Harvard University Press, 1960

Bruner, J.S. "The Act of Discovery." *Harvard Educational Review* 31 (1961): 21-32.

Copi, I. *Introduction to Logic (5th ed.).* New York: Macmillan, 1978.

Davidson, J.E., and Sternberg, R.J. "The Role of Insight in Intellectual Giftedness." *Gifted Child Quarterly* 28 (1984): 58-64.

de Bono, E. *The Five-Day Course in Thinking.* Harmondsworth, England: Penguin, 1967.

de Bono, E. *The Mechanism of Mind.* New York: Simon and Schuster, 1969.

Ennis, R.H. "What is Critical Thinking?" In *Teaching Thinking Skills: Theory and Practice.* New York: Freeman, in press.

Ennis, R.H., and Millman, J. *The Cornell Critical Thinking Test.* Urbana, Ill.: Critical Thinking Project, 1971.

Feuerstein, R. *Instrumental Enrichment: An Intervention Program for Cognition Modifiability.* Baltimore: University Park Press, 1980.

Gagne, R.M. "Learning Aspects of Problem Solving." *Educational Psychologist* 15 (1980): 84-92.

Gubbins, E.J. "Matrix of Thinking Skills" (unpublished document). Hartford, Conn.: State Department of Education, 1985.

Guyote, M.J., and Sternberg, R.J. "A Transitive-Chain Theory of Syllogistic Reasoning." *Cognitive Psychology* 13 (1981): 461-525.

Lipman, M. *Harry Stottlemeir's Discovery.* Upper Montclair, N.J.: Montclair State College Press, 1974.

Lipman, M., and Sharp, A.M., eds. *Instructional Manual to Accompany Harry Stottlemeir's Discovery.* Upper Montclair, N.J.: Montclair State College, Institute for the Advancement of Philosophy for Children, 1975.

Lipman, M. "Some Thoughts on the Foundations of Reflective Thinking." In *Teaching Thinking Skills: Theory and Practice.* Edited by J.B. Baron and R.J. Sternberg. New York: Freeman, in press.

Lipman, M.; Sharp, A.M.; and Oscanyan, F.S. *Philosophy in the Classroom.* Upper Montclair, N.J.: Institute for the Advancement of Philosophy for Children, 1977.

Nickerson, R.S.; Perkins, D.N.; and Smith, E.E. *Teaching Thinking.* Hillsdale, N.J.: Erlbaum, in press.

Paul, R. "Dialogical Thinking: Critical Thought Essential to the Acquisition of Rational Knowledge and Passions." In *Teaching Thinking Skills: Theory and Practice.* Edited by J.B. Baron and R.J. Sternberg. New York: Freeman, in press

Perkins, D. *The Mind's Best Work.* Cambridge: Harvard University Press, 1981.

Renzulli, J.S. "The Enrichment Triad Model: A Guide for Developing Defensible Programs for the Gifted and Talented." *Gifted Child Quarterly* 20 (1976): 303-326.

Shipman, V. *New Jersey Test of Reasoning Skills, Form B.* Upper Montclair, N.J.: Montclair State College, 1983.

Sternberg, R.J. *Beyond IQ: A Triarchic Theory of Human Intelligence.* New York: Cambridge University Press, 1985.

Sternberg, R.J. *Intelligence Applied: Understanding and Increasing Your Intellectual Skills.* San Diego: Harcourt, Brace, Jovanovich, 1986.

Sternberg, R.J. "Teaching Critical Thinking: Are We Making Critical Mistakes?" *Phi Delta Kappan*, in press.

Sternberg, R.J. and Davidson, J.E. "Insight in the Gifted." *Educational Psychologist* 18 (1983): 52-58.

Wagner, R.K., and Sternberg, R.J. "Alternative Conceptions of Intelligence and Their Implications for Education." *Review of Educational Research* 54 (1984): 197-224.

Watson, G., and Glaser, E.M. *Watson-Glaser Critical Thinking Appraisal.* New York: Harcourt, Brace, Jovanovich, 1980.

Whimbey, A., and Lochhead, J. *Problem Solving and Comprehension: A Short Course in Analytic Reasoning.* Philadelphia: Franklin Institute Press, 1982.

4. Thinking and Writing

Allan A. Glatthorn

NOW IS AN APPROPRIATE TIME TO REFLECT ABOUT THE RELATIONSHIP between thinking and writing. The interest in the teaching of writing continues unabated, and the interest in the teaching of thinking, as this volume attests, seems to be increasing. This chapter, therefore, attempts to examine what is known about that relationship and to discuss its educational implications.

The Relationship Between Thinking and Writing

How are thinking and writing related? According to Berthoff (1978), "learning to write is a way of learning to think and . . . thinking requires knowing how to discover and put to use the resources of language" (p. 10). That apposite summation, however, obscures a more complex relationship, which requires some further analysis. That analysis perhaps can be facilitated by asking two closely related questions: What is the relationship of writing to thinking, and what is the relationship of thinking to writing? Although the processes are closely and interactively related, the two different perspectives might yield some useful insights.

How Is Writing Related to Thinking?

As one of the most important systems of symbols, writing serves as an instrument of thinking. According to Piaget (1952), we think in symbols. In his view, thinking is essentially a process of evoking a symbol into active memory and putting it into relation with another symbol. That belief, that all thinking is essentially symbolic, however, is now generally questioned by cognitive psychologists and epistemologists. Bishop (1983), for example, makes this point quite strongly: "Our experience of non-deliberative, intentional action shows, *prima facie*, that we do not do all our thinking in language" (p. 14). Most, however, would still agree that conscious, deliberative thought makes extensive use of symbols as a representation of reflection.

The nature of the symbolic representation, Vygotsky (1978) points out, follows a developmental path: the child first symbolizes with verbal language and make-believe play, then with drawings, and finally with written language. Thus language in general and writing in particular serve an instrumental function: we speak and write as a result of thinking, as a basic means of changing thought into action.

Written language, however, is not solely an instrument of thought. It plays an important facilitative and shaping role in the development of two aspects of thinking. It first of all seems to be essential in the development of the ability to think propositionally. Here a distinction made by Bruner (1975) seems most useful. He distinguishes between "communicative competence," the ability to think and communicate about concrete reality, and "analytic competence," which involves the operation of thinking processes on language and propositional structures free of the concrete context. Written language plays a key role in the development of communicative competence, obviously; it seems especially important, however, in the development and application of analytic competence. The special nature of writing seems to distance us from concrete reality and facilitates the analysis of those propositional structures. Its linear and structured form imposes its own sense of order on our attempts to think about relationships. And, as "frozen speech," it makes meta-linguistic reflection more easily accomplished.

In understanding how writing facilitates the development of analytic competence, it is useful to think of writing as one of the "distancing behaviors," to use a concept that Sigel (1984) has given us. As Sigel uses the term, distancing behaviors are "a class of events which create demands on the individual to engage in activities such as planning, reconstructing, anticipating, predicting, and the like" (p. 12). Sigel's research suggests that these distancing behaviors create a set of antecedent conditions that facilitate the development of representational thought. So as students grapple with a challenging writing task, they are required to reconstruct knowledge, plan the communication, and shape the message. Thus, they become separated or distanced from the concrete reality of the present—a requisite for the development of analytic competence.

Perhaps in a more important way writing seems to play a unique role in facilitating what Polanyi (1966) calls *tacit knowing*, the deeply personal knowledge that lies beneath conscious awareness. We gain access to that tacit knowledge by grappling and struggling with a problem whose solution is indeterminate. And the act of writing, in a way that makes it significantly different from the act of speaking, is essentially an exploration into the unknown: we write to discover what we know. The desire to write becomes a need to discern order and make connections. Here again Berthoff (1979) is most apposite: "It is the discursive, generalizing, forming power of language which makes meaning from chaos" (p. 5).

How Is Thinking Related to Writing?

Thus thinking uses and is facilitated by writing. How does writing make use of thinking? Although we are not sure of the details of the process, there are several cognitively oriented models that provide a general picture of the relationship between writing and thinking. Perhaps the most useful of these is that provided by Flower and Hayes (1980). Their model of the composing process, somewhat simplified, embodies these components:

● The writer engages with a task environment—a rhetorical problem of saying something to an audience for a specified purpose. That engagement provides a framework for all that follows.

● In response to that task environment, the writer draws from long-term memory two types of information: knowledge of topic and audience and knowledge of writing plans. This act of retrieval is usually part of what others call "pre-writing."

● By using that information, the writer generates plans—setting goals and organizing knowledge to achieve those goals. Plan-setting is also usually considered an aspect of pre-writing.

● The writer translates or transcribes the information and plans into written words, producing a text that becomes an added part of the task environment. Now the writer not only has to attend to the original rhetorical problem; he or she has to respond to what has already been written. This is the drafting stage, to use more conventional terminology.

● The writer reviews what has been written, first evaluating and then editing in response to the evaluation. The evaluation and editing are the closely related aspects of the revision stage.

• The writer monitors the generating, the translating, and the reviewing—reflecting, assessing, and making corrections. The monitoring goes on throughout all three stages—pre-writing, drafting, revising.

Although presented here in a linear sequence, the writing process, as Flower and Hayes and other theorists conceive it, is interactive and recursive: the writer draws information from memory throughout all stages of the process, generates and revises plans in the act of translating or drafting, and begins to review and revise when the first sentence has been written. Throughout this recursive process, thinking is at the center—in retrieving information from memory, in generating plans, in reviewing, and, most critically, in monitoring the entire process.

However, even the best of the writing process models leave us with many unanswered questions, to which an increasing body of research has still not supplied answers. After reviewing all the recent research on writing and thinking, Larson (1983, pp. 250-251) identifies these unanswered questions:

1. How does the impulse to write arise?

2. How does a writer arrive at a perspective, an approach to the subject?

3. Once a writer has defined a "rhetorical problem," how does he or she go about solving it?

4. How does the writer, having invented concepts and perceptions, defined a problem, and formulated a plan, find language in which to embody these decisions?

5. What is the role of feelings, intuitions, cognitively indescribable impulses and acts, in the arrangement of language?

This rather comprehensive list suggests quite convincingly that we do not really know much about the particulars of the writing-thinking connection. We are left only with a somewhat platitudinous generalization: good writing requires good thinking.

The Educational Implications of the Relationship

So thinking and writing are closely interrelated, in ways we do not fully understand. What are the educational implications of such a close linkage? The answer perhaps can best be understood by examining the issue again from two perspectives: How can writing be used to facilitate thinking? How can our knowledge of thinking be used to improve writing?

How Can Writing Be Used to Facilitate Thinking?

If writing indeed has a special role to play in the development of thinking, then it would follow that writing should be emphasized in programs that teach thinking. However, before examining this issue in some detail, it might be useful to raise a caution about the over-emphasis of writing as an aspect of thinking.

There are admittedly some dangers in giving writing too central a role in teaching thinking and in urging teachers to emphasize writing in all school subjects, as some have recently done. All students should learn to use both verbal and nonverbal methods for perceiving a problem, representing knowledge, and reporting a solution; over-emphasizing writing might impede the development of nonverbal abilities. Some thinking skills do not seem to be primarily verbal in nature. For example, the process of choosing a strategy for solving a problem, identified by Sternberg (1983) as one of the essential "executive processes," would not seem to require or be especially facilitated by writing. And students who do not have strong verbal abilities should not be penalized by being required to use only verbal processes in solving problems or learning academic content. Students need variety in their educational programs: emphasizing writing in every course runs the risk of making the industrial arts shop another version of English class.

With those cautions in mind, however, it does make sense to give writing appropriate attention in the development of thinking skills. Let us first examine to what extent currently available programs emphasize thinking, and then consider what local districts might do on their own.

In reviewing currently available programs, it becomes evident that there is relatively little attention to writing as an aspect of thinking. In his recent review of critical thinking programs, Nickerson (1984) notes that "the idea that thinking can be improved through instruction in writing has been promoted more in books than in programs" (p. 18)—and then lists only a few writing and language arts texts. He does note, however, that programs like LOGO, which teach students how to write computer programs, should be considered a special type of writing program that teaches thinking.

My own review tends to bear out Nickerson's impression. Of all the programs I have examined, only Lipman's Philosophy for Children seems to give explicit attention to writing; one of his secondary curriculum units, *Suki*, deals with the obstacles young people have in writing poetry and fiction, and its main character, Suki, is a youngster who finds meaning by writing poetry. In Lipman's view, however, writing seems to be of secondary importance to talking. In his discussion of the theoretical foundations for his Philosophy for Children program, Lipman (1984) emphasizes talking, not writing: "For educational purposes, the behavioral matrix of thinking is *talking*, and the matrix of organized thinking, i.e., reasoning, is *organized talking*" (p. 7).

However, in other widely used approaches, writing receives at best minimal attention. In Parnes' Creative Problem Solving (Parnes, Noller, and Biondi, 1977), in Whimbey and Lochhead's (1981) cognitive process instruction, and in Wales and Stager's (1977) "guided design," writing is presented only as one of many culminating activities, not as a process central to problem solving.

But the depreciation of writing as an aspect of thinking is most marked in de Bono's CoRT Thinking program. In his *CoRT Teachers Notes*, de Bono offers this advice in describing the standard lesson format:

The output from the groups is almost always verbal. If the teacher feels that the groups are not happy with verbal output because their ideas are not getting through an output in written note form can be used in addition. Where the teacher feels that a particular group is being lazy and not bothering to tackle the items a note form output can be demanded from the group (1973, p. 30).

Although an "English essay" is recommended as an optional "project activity," de Bono for the most part emphasizes writing only as "output in written note form," something that is demanded from lazy groups. Or, as my 5th grade teacher often told me, "If you don't behave, you'll have to write."

Thus it would seem that writing as a means of facilitating thinking has been minimized by most of the leaders in the field of critical thinking and creative problem solving. The issue, however, has received much recent attention by leaders of the "writing across the curriculum" movement, who argue that writing should play a key role in facilitating learning—and thus thinking—in all the disciplines. Perhaps the most cogent theoretical arguments have been advanced by Yinger and Clark (1981), who offer seven reasons for the centrality of writing in the learning process: writing is integrative, entailing the active use of one's total intellectual equipment; writing requires symbol manipulation, which in turn facilitates learning; writing serves an epistemic function, modifying the human knowledge it records; writing is a unique mode of learning, involving all the major types of learning; writing provides both immediate and long-term self-provided feedback; writing is active and personal; and writing is a self-paced mode of learning.

The promise suggested in these theoretical arguments for writing across the curriculum unfortunately has not been often realized in practice. My review of the literature of that field suggests that most "writing across the curriculum" projects give only scant attention to the cognitive processes that should play a central role when writing is used as a way of learning. Reports of such projects suggest that too many are unduly concerned with teaching students how to write the term paper and take notes from lectures.

There are, however, some important exceptions, noted here briefly since they would seem to have direct implications for the teaching of thinking. Weiss and his colleagues (1980) ask students to clarify, articulate, and confirm their own learning by stating in writing the concepts they have learned. Suppose, for example, that students are discussing in political science class how lobbyists operate. The teacher might say to the class, "Write in your notebooks a few sentences explaining how lobbyists actually function as an 'invisible legislature.'" Note that this strategy is significantly different from the usual classroom note-taking; the student is expected to synthesize and generalize, not simply copy.

Fulwiler (1978) encourages teachers to have students in all subjects keep journals or intellectual diaries in which they record their questions about what has been taught, their feelings and values as they reflect about concepts and issues, and their ideas for applying what they have learned. Wotring (1980) reported mixed success with using journals in high school chemistry: students seemed to need a great deal of help in keeping and learning from their journals.

One of the most promising strategies is that advocated by Giroux (1979). He encourages teachers to develop writing lessons that help students understand and apply the inquiry skills important in their discipline. One exercise he developed for a high school social studies class, for example, helps students think and write about the historian's "frame of reference," a key concept in historiography.

Note the irony implicit in the situation described above: programs designed to teach thinking slight the use of writing; programs designed to use writing as a way of learning give scant attention to thinking. How can a more appropriate balance be achieved? What can local districts do to help teachers use writing to facilitate thinking and learning? The answer, obviously, will depend upon the general approach the school adopts in teaching critical thinking.

There will be some schools that will adopt existing programs, like the ones cited above. In such a case, we can show teachers how to strengthen the writing component, wherever that seems appropriate. Thus, if we teach one of de Bono's strategies, taking another person's point of view (what he calls OPV), we could wisely move writing to a more central place, presenting the students with a task like this one:

Suppose that the school board in your district is considering reducing the summer vacation by two weeks. Students, teachers, and citizens have been asked to write letters to the president of the board expressing their points of view. Write three letters. One letter should be from you and express your point of view. A second letter should be written as if a teacher has written it, expressing a teacher's point of view. And the third letter should be written as if a member of the community has written it, expressing his or her point of view.

Some schools will choose to write their own curricular materials, either for separate courses in thinking and problem solving or for special units and lessons in existing courses. In such a case the curriculum planners should be sure that writing is given appropriate but not excessive attention. Suppose, for example, that one of the curriculum units is designed to teach students how to represent information about a problem, another of Sternberg's "executive processes." The unit should provide opportunities for the student to understand, apply, and evaluate several different methods of representing information: oral language, written language, mathematical notation, figural or graphic forms. We do not suggest that writing is the best method. Neither do we simply cite it in passing as a supplementary project. We help the student understand the special uses and limitations of written language as one means of representing information.

My own preference is for a staff development program that helps teachers understand how to teach thinking and writing skills in their own disciplines. It is a classroom-centered approach that recognizes that in an important sense the teacher is the curriculum. In working with teachers at several levels in different disciplines, I have had some success in teaching them to use a process that I call "modeling the good student-thinker" (Glatthorn, 1984). Let me describe briefly each step in the process and for each note an example.

1. *Select a concept or skill that you ordinarily teach.* Let's suppose an English teacher of an advanced placement class decides to teach this skill: evaluating a poem.

2. *Identify the thought processes that play an important role as the student tries to understand that concept or develop that skill.* Identify these processes first by analyzing your own thinking. How would you evaluate a poem? Then reflect about the thought processes of your students. At their stage of development, how do they think? Discuss with other teachers your own and your students' thought processes.

Through these steps, you are developing your own model of "the good student-thinker."

By following these guidelines, the English teacher might develop this model of the good student-thinker evaluating a poem:

–Reads the poem and responds to it personally, without worrying initially about evaluation.

–Reads the poem a second time, being especially sensitive to interpretive insights.

–Identifies the type of poem; considers the criteria important in evaluating poetry in general and poems of that particular genre.

–Uses those criteria in re-reading the poem and making tentative judgments about the quality of the poem.

–Systematizes the judgments made and prepares to document them.

3. By reviewing the model of the "good student-thinker," and by reflecting about student learning styles, *develop a tentative plan for a lesson or unit that would teach those thought processes.*

The English teacher might develop a one-week unit in poetry evaluation that at first would provide students with guided experiences in using that model and would then let students use the model (or their own version of it) without teacher direction.

4. Based upon your knowledge of those students and those processes, determine when and how writing could best be used. *Build appropriate writing activities into your lesson materials.* The teacher might decide at this juncture to have students do three types of writing activities: they respond personally in their journals; they write their own initial evaluations, without worrying unduly about criteria or documentation; they write an evaluative essay that systematizes and documents their reflective evaluations.

5. *Try out your lesson materials, modify them as necessary, and share them with your colleagues.* The teacher tries out the materials, finds that students need more help in referring to the poem to support their evaluations, and modifies the materials accordingly.

Predictably, the results of teaching teachers the "good student-thinker" model are somewhat uneven. Some of the materials seem excellent: the materials focus on a concept or skill that the teachers consider important, explicate the related thinking skills, provide appropriate learning activities, and make effective use of writing. Others are unimaginative refurbishings of standard lessons with a little thinking and writing thrown in: "What would you have done if you had been with Columbus? Brainstorm, and then write a diary entry."

Yet even when the products have been somewhat disappointing, the process seems to have been productive. By reflecting about their own thinking processes and by modeling the good student-thinker, teachers report that they have learned a great deal about teaching critical thinking. The staff development program becomes for them a distancing context, with its own cognitive demands.

So writing in special ways facilitates thinking—and warrants appropriate attention in programs designed to teach thinking.

How Can Our Knowledge of Thinking Be Used to Facilitate Writing?

We turn our attention now to the other perspective about the educational implications, the rather complex matter of improving writing by drawing on our knowledge of thinking. Perhaps the issue can best be examined by posing and attempting to answer several specific questions subsumed under the more general one.

1. To what extent should our knowledge of cognition influence our approach to writing?

This, of course, is the fundamental question whose answer informs all others. There are many in the field who would seem to minimize the contributions of cognitive psychology to the teaching of writing. Clifford (1984) makes the following observation in assessing the contribution of cognitive psychology to this field:

This is not to say that cognitive psychologists do not say things we should pay attention to. They are not irrelevant. They know how to get things done. And many of their findings corroborate the best of our intuitive feelings about composing. But somehow, after all their models and sub-processes, we have learned surprisingly little that we did not already know. Composition theorists are hoping to build a comprehensive framework that tries to relate reader, writer, and text within the social, philosophical, and psychological matrix of the classroom. For that effort, cognitive psychology appears ready to make but a minor contribution (p. 18).

And many leaders in the field seem to advocate a method of teaching writing that minimizes explicit attention to the thought processes. Elbow (1975 and 1981) recommends an approach that might be capsulized in this manner: create a supportive environment for writing; encourage students to write freely about their beliefs and feelings; have them read and respond to each other's writing; don't worry about teaching writing or thinking skills.

On the other hand, there are those like Odell (1983) who believe that student writers can profit from explicit attention to intellectual processes. By analyzing both professional and student writing from the perspective of tagmemic theory, Odell was able to identify these processes as playing an important role in effective professional writing: variation in focus, contrast, classification, change, reference to sequence, and reference to physical context. And he provides some useful illustrations of how students can be taught to use those same processes in exploring and communicating ideas.

Rather than choosing between a free writing and a cognitively oriented process, I have advocated developing a composition program that gives appropriate attention to each (Glatthorn, 1981). Part of the composition program would emphasize what I term an "organic" writing approach. The organic program is essentially like the one Elbow advocates: students are encouraged to write personally and imaginatively in a supportive workshop environment; they are told to write freely, without being concerned with forms and rules; they share their writing with each other, with very little correction by the teacher. In the organic program there is no explicit attention given to thinking and writing skills. It is a student-centered approach that places primary value on authentic feeling and fluent writing.

And part of the writing program emphasizes a "mastery" approach. In the mastery approach the teacher presents the students with a variety of communication problems, does a task analysis of the thinking and writing skills involved in solving that problem, teaches those skills, and assesses the final product to determine to what extent those skills have been used effectively. The mastery approach emphasizes careful analysis, planned teaching, and systematic assessment. It places primary value on the effective solving of a problem in communication.

The optimal balance between the organic and the mastery approach for a particular grade level and for different types of students is a matter that is perhaps best determined by district curriculum specialists and classroom teachers. However, perhaps some general guidelines can be offered here. The literature on children's learning and the recommendations of experts would suggest that the elementary program should emphasize an organic approach. As Vygotsky (1978) notes, the young child should learn to write "as a natural moment in her development" (p. 118). In the middle school grades the program might devote about equal attention to both an organic and a mastery approach; the learner is now ready for the more formal and more systematic thrust of the mastery program—but frequent opportunities for the organic component should still be provided. At the high school level there is probably more warrant for emphasizing a mastery approach, stressing the types of writing expected in college and on the job.

Similar variations could be justified for students with different levels of motivation and verbal ability. The testimony of experienced teachers suggests that the organic approach seems more intrinsically interesting to students who are reluctant to write and deficient in writing skills; such students seem to respond more positively to an approach that emphasizes personal writing and peer responding. However, I do not know of any persuasive body of empirical evidence to support this or any other answer to the issue of curricular balance.

2. To what extent should our knowledge of cognitive development affect the organization of the writing curriculum?

Many experts have answered this question by arguing for a close linkage between the two. Some have taken what might be termed a strict Piagetian stance. For example, Amiran and Mann (1982) assert quite strongly that the structure and sequence of writing assignments should be designed in view of the students' cognitive development: "Paragraph writing which calls for the child to assess the audience's viewpoint cannot be demanded of children who have not yet transcended their original egocentrism" (p. 50). And Odell (1973), among others, has developed a writing curriculum and a sequence of assignments that reflect a Piagetian perspective.

Others have recommended a more flexible approach, usually citing Vygotsky's (1979) theory of proximal development. The zone of proximal development, in Vygotsky's formulation, is "the distance between the actual developmental level as determined by independent problem solving and the level of potential development as determined through problem solving under adult guidance or in collaboration with more capable peers" (p. 86). Vygotsky argued that learning at its best creates the zone of proximal development, awakening more advanced developmental processes that operate only when the child interacts with adults and peers in a stimulating environment. From this viewpoint a good writing assignment would challenge youngsters to think and write in the zone of proximal development.

This more flexible approach seems to be a wiser stance for curriculum planners and teachers to take. The problems inherent in a rigid application of simplistic notions about cognitive development can perhaps best be illustrated by examining the issue of how to sequence the types of writing. Those who seem to have a superficial understanding of cognitive development advance an argument that might be paraphrased in this manner:

Children at the stage of concrete operations (roughly ages 2-11) are egocentric; they cannot decenter or take the roles of others. Since argumentation and persuasion require decentering and role-taking, those types of writing should not be introduced until the child has reached the stage of formal operations (roughly ages 11-15). Emphasize argumentation in high school, when the student has mastered role-taking.

The empirical evidence would not support such a doctrinaire position. To begin with, many highly respected cognitive psychologists are questioning the basic assumptions of stage theory. After reviewing recent evidence, Gelman and Baillargeon (1983) conclude that "there is very little evidence to support the idea of major stages in cognitive development of the type described by Piaget" (p. 214), noting that even the "pre-operational child" has much more competence than ordinarily expected. Several research studies indicate that younger children can produce a simple form of persuasive discourse—and their persuasive writing is more syntactically complex than their narratives. (See, for example, Perron, 1977.) And Scardamalia, Bereiter, and McDonald (1977) found that problems with role-taking persisted until grade 11 at least—and significantly affected the quality of writing.

Thus, the evidence would question the wisdom of postponing all persuasive writing until secondary school and then expecting the adolescent to have mastered the complex intellectual skills required. It would seem wiser to provide the developing learner with a variety of writing experiences at all levels, hold reasonable expectations for performance, and remain sensitive to individual differences.

3. What kind of classroom environment will be most conducive to the development of writing and thinking skills?

The research on teacher effectiveness provides a general picture of the type of classroom environment that for most students will result in higher achievement on the standard academic measures: the teacher plays a central role in setting and enforcing limits for behavior; the teacher sets reasonably high expectations for the students; the teacher provides a clear organizing structure for verbal learning, identifying objectives, explicating concepts, and modeling skills; the teacher provides opportunities for guided and independent practice; the teacher monitors behavior and keeps students on task; the teacher assesses learning and provides appropriate feedback. (See, for example, my 1984 review and critique of this research.)

While this task-oriented and highly structured environment seems appropriate for acquisition of the basic skills whose mastery is usually equated with "achievement," there is a body of theory and research that would question it as the best environment for learning to write and think. It might be useful, therefore, to call special attention here to the ways in which the writing classroom, one where thinking is encouraged, would be significantly different from this standard prescription.

First, there would probably be more social interaction and peer cooperation. Bruffee (1984) points out quite cogently that writing, though often performed in isolation, is essentially a social and collaborative act, best nurtured in an environment in which dialogue is encouraged and cooperation is rewarded: "In order to learn to write, we must learn to become our own representatives of an assenting community of peers with whom we speak and to whom we listen in our heads" (p. 168). He reports continued success in using peer groups to facilitate the thinking and writing processes, and several studies support the conclusion that peer interaction is especially useful during the pre-writing and revising stages. (See Amiran and Mann's 1982 review.)

Next, the teacher would place more emphasis on the solving of thinking and communicating problems, and less on the explication of content. Most experts would agree with Kroll's (1979) argument for the need for a problem-solving environment. Since intellectual growth takes place best of all when a person interacts with the environment, one of the teacher's essential functions is to structure communication contexts that provide the student with a real problem to solve, a genuine purpose in writing, and an audience other than the teacher.

Third, the learning activities would probably be more diversified and intellectually engaging. Typically, in the teacher-centered classroom where direct instruction is emphasized, the student plays a role that critics usually characterize as "passive"—listening, reading, answering teacher questions, writing answers to practice exercises. In the best thinking-writing environment, if we are to believe the reports of successful teachers, the student plays a quite different role as a learner—fantasizing, meditating, talking, asking questions, observing, acting parts, and creating novel solutions. While all of us are not happy with the tendency to characterize such methods as being designed for the "right brain," most would agree on the need for more emphasis on intuition and imagination.

Finally, there would be a different attitude toward error. In the conventional classroom, error is usually perceived as inherently bad and something to be extirpated. As Kroll and Shaefer (1977) note, current theory and research on cognition and language suggest a quite different view: errors are natural; they arise from the learner's active strategies to master language; they are the result of a misguided but rule-based system; they are important to the teacher and the student, since they provide data useful in the formulation of more appropriate rules. Such a view informed the seminal work of Mina Shaughnessy (1977), whose work with "basic writers" provided both an intellectual grounding and a professional impetus for the current work in error analysis.

4. What types of teaching/learning activities should be used to facilitate the pre-writing stage?

The term *pre-writing* seems to be an unfortunate one, since its etymology suggests activities that take place before the drafting stage; for most effective writers, those activities usually subsumed under the term (such as generating ideas, retrieving information, and making plans) actually continue throughout the writing process, not just at the beginning. However, the term is so widely used and accepted in the profession that it makes sense to use it as a general label for the following thinking/writing operations:

- Finding a reason to write.
- Finding something to say—choosing a focus.
- Generating ideas.
- Retrieving the information needed—from the environment, from long-term memory, from computers and books.
- Reflecting about the intended audience—their prior knowledge and their expectations.
- Making tentative decisions about selection, order, and emphasis.
- Reflecting about tone, rehearsing the voice.
- Analyzing the special nature of the chosen medium and its effects on the message.

Those operations overlap, of course, and do not occur in linear fashion, despite the fact that many composition textbooks still pretend that they do. They are, however, vitally important: the research is conclusive that giving attention to these operations will improve writing. (See Humes' 1983 review for a useful summary.)

What kind of attention seems to be most productive? A shift in the nature of the answers to this question is discernible. For several years most teachers of writing seemed greatly influenced by the early work of D. Gordon Rohman (1965). Rohman's investigations persuaded him that pre-writing techniques should be primarily concerned with stimulating the creative process; he recommended that student writers should keep journals, practice meditation, and use analogies. Other teachers, like Peter Elbow (1975), believed that creative thinking and writing could be facilitated by "free writing"—writing discursively about one's feelings and ideas, without concern for form.

During the 1970s there seemed to be greater interest in teaching students to use heuristics, strategies for generating ideas. Corbett (1971) updated the "invention" strategies of classical rhetoric; Young, Becker, and Pike (1970) drew from Pike's work in tagmemic theory; Irmscher's (1972) text leaned heavily on Kenneth Burke's "pentad." It might be noted here that the extensive use of the computer in the classroom seems to have revived interest in heuristics; several software programs attempt to facilitate the pre-writing process through interactive heuristics.

At the present time there seems to be greater interest in both experiential and cognitive approaches to pre-writing. The experiential approaches are based on the assumption that writing at its best derives from real experience and attempts to solve actual problems; thus, the function of pre-writing, from this perspective, is to provide an experiential stimulus and context for communication. Hillocks (1979), for example, found that structuring observational activities resulted in better writing.

The cognitive approaches give more explicit attention to the mental operations important in planning and writing. Flower's (1981) text, which draws from her research into the composing process, teaches students how to construe writing as a problem-solving activity; it places much emphasis on the cognitive processes important in developing and carrying out plans. Others recommend the use of what might be termed "thinking activities"—classroom lessons designed to foster the development of cognitive processes. Johannessen, Kahn, and Walter (1982) recommend teaching these thinking skills during the pre-writing stage: identifying and defining a problem, gathering data, classifying, differentiating, relating examples to given criteria, formulating clear criteria, generating examples from experience or inventing hypothetical cases, analyzing borderline cases, clarifying limits of a term. Their pilot study suggested that teaching those skills was more effective than using models and warm-up activities. Although such concern for thinking skills seems appropriate, de Beaugrande's (1984) caution should be noted here: too much stress upon logic can inhibit the creative learning processes.

Rather than arguing for one particular approach over another, it perhaps makes more sense to understand how these different strategies complement each other. As indicated in Figure 4.1, they might

Figure 4.1. A Synthesis of Pre-Writing Strategies	
Purpose	*Strategies*
1. To become open to one's intuitions, insights, and experiences.	Meditation Fantasy Journal-keeping Free writing
2. To generate ideas.	Heuristics Observing
3. To develop cognitive operations necessary for ordering and communicating experience.	"Thinking" activities
4. To develop and implement plans for writing.	Making sketches Mapping

best be characterized in terms of their communication purpose. And the choice of a particular strategy would be determined by analyzing the purpose considered most important for a given group of students confronting a particular type of communication problem.

Consider some examples that illustrate this point. One teacher has a group of reluctant teenage students who are expected to write about a personal experience. The teacher uses a guided fantasy as the key pre-writing activity. Another teacher is working with a group of managers who are trying to learn how to write an effective memo; that teacher uses one of Flower's problem-solving and planning strategies in the pre-writing period. A third teacher wants college-bound seniors to learn how to write an evaluative essay; she emphasizes the cognitive processes of classifying, setting criteria, and judging.

All are using quite different pre-writing strategies—but each approach would seem to be effective for that group of students and that task.

5. How can our knowledge of cognitive processes be used to facilitate and support the drafting stage?

Drafting is the term usually given to the physical act of writing, of transcribing and translating ideas into written text. From the perspective of this chapter, its chief characteristic is that it is marked by what some have called cognitive overload. At any particular moment the writer is dealing with these demands: moving the piece of writing ahead by focusing on an idea; retrieving information from long-term memory; choosing the words that will best convey the message; making tentative choices of syntactic and sentence forms; remembering the written form of the word; engaging in the motor behaviors of writing; using the conventional devices for segmenting prose; monitoring what has been written. As others have noted, anyone who reflects objectively about the complexity of writing is amazed that it ever gets done at all.

The conventional advice for dealing with the cognitive overload of the drafting period is, "Forget about matters of word choice and form—just get your ideas down on paper." Obviously there is some merit in this suggestion for students who can free themselves from worrying about spelling and punctuation until they have finished the first draft. Howver, as Scardamalia (1981) notes, many of the students who have the most difficulty with spelling and punctuation are just the ones who can't stop fretting about those matters. They may need some specific help from the teacher in reducing the overload.

How can the overload be reduced? Robert de Beaugrande (1984) offers a comprehensive list of strategies that derive from his own theory of text production. Let me list some of them here, paraphrasing liberally in order to avoid using some of his own special terminology:

- Reschedule time in order to slow down the process.
- Relax your demands on yourself—be satisfied with some inept phrasing until there is more time to polish.
- Reduce syntactic complexity by using simpler clauses and sentences.
- Deal first with general issues and then return to add details.
- Increase and tolerate redundancy by using more expressions to convey the same idea (as we do in conversation).
- Increase concentration by consciously focusing attention.
- Repeat part of the task, using prior results as guidelines.
- Stretch out some of the operations, so that instead of trying to handle them all at once, they are dealt with successively.

Here again the pedagogical answer would seem to be one of enlightened flexibility. Teachers should be encouraged to become their own researchers, observing and analyzing how their students learn in general and how they deal with the writing process in particular. Some student writers will be helped with reassurance: "Spelling doesn't count; make up your own spelling." Some will be helped by being taught some useful formulas: "Use this strategy for organizing a memo." Many will profit from on-the-spot peer assistance: "If you need to spell a word, ask our Class Spellers."

Finally, it should be noted here that the drafting stage is greatly facilitated, for many student writers, through the use of word processors. (See, for example, Collins 1983.)

6. How can our knowledge of thinking and writing be used in facilitating the revision process?

Revision is a complex process. It involves two related operations—evaluating what one has written and modifying the text as a result of those evaluations. It occurs at several levels—the writer revises a word, a phrase, a sentence, a paragraph, and the order and content of the whole text. And it occurs within drafts and between drafts.

How do writers handle these processes? The research provides some tentative answers, although it would be unwise to generalize too much here. (The collection of papers edited by Sudol, 1982, is perhaps the best current source for a synthesis of that research.) In general, skilled writers revise as they write, focusing their attention on the larger elements of order, content, and structure. Or, as Witte and Faigley (1981) note, they produce more effective revisions because they are concerned with the "macrostructure" of the piece of writing.

Unskilled writers tend to be of two sorts. Some might be termed "obsessive correctors." They fuss inordinately with spelling and punctuation, worrying unduly that they have repeated a word or forgotten a comma. Others might be called "compulsive finishers." They rush through the writing assignment, oblivious to mistakes, and impatiently ask, "Do I have to write it over in ink?" The unskilled writer's insensitivity to error may be related to the genesis of such error. Daiute (1982) hypothesizes that sentence errors result in this fashion; the writer completes a "perceptual clause" (a noun/verb pair), erases it from short-term memory, stores it in long-term memory, remembers the meaning but not the exact words, and then writes the next piece in a way that does not link syntactically with the first. Daiute notes that most usage and sentence errors occur when the writer is more than seven words into the sentence, and relates this finding to the fact that only seven units can be held in short-term memory.

A review of the theory and research on revision would suggest that the following instructional strategies would be useful in teaching both skilled and unskilled writers:

1. Create a writing environment in which revision is expected and valued.

2. Teach student writers how to revise within drafts, focusing on the macrostructure of what they have written.

3. Set up peer response groups. Help students understand the difference between responding as an appreciative audience and correcting as an editor. Teach them how to give and profit from both responses.

4. Do not grade initial drafts; instead give students constructive feedback between drafts.

5. Do not require every paper to be revised. In some cases the writer is working at the performance ceiling, and the paper should be accepted in its imperfect state; in some cases the writing should be considered a work in progress, put aside for later rethinking; and in some cases the results are so unsatisfactory that the writer should discard what has been written and start all over again.

Again, word processors are playing an important role here. They simplify self-editing, and many include text-editor programs that make the task even easier.

In summary, then, the profession stands at an interesting juncture. The current interest in the teaching of thinking can build upon and extend what is already known about the teaching of writing. It seems reasonable to hope that the coalescence of interests will result in students who can think more rationally and write more effectively.

References

Amiran, E., and Mann, J. *Written Composition, Grades K-12: Literature Synthesis and Report.* Portland, Ore.: Northwest Regional Educational Laboratory, 1982.

Berthoff, A.E. *Forming/Thinking/Writing: The Composing Imagination.* Montclair, N.J.: Boynton/Cook, 1978.

Berthoff, A.E. "Learning the Uses of Chaos." Paper presented at the meeting of the Canadian Council of Teachers of English, Ottawa, May 1979.

Bishop, J. "Can There Be Thought Without Language?" In *Thinking: The Expanding Frontier.* Edited by W. Maxwell. Philadelphia: Franklin Institute, 1983.

Bruffee, K.A. "Writing and Reading as Collaborative or Social Acts." In *The Writer's Mind: Writing as a Mode of Thinking.* Edited by J.N. Hays, P.A. Roth, J.R. Ramsey, and R.D. Foulke. Urbana, Ill.: National Council of Teachers of English, 1984.

Bruner, J.S. "Language as an Instrument of Thought." In *Problems of Language and Learning.* Edited by A. Davies. London: Heinemann, 1975.

Clifford, J. "Cognitive Psychology and Writing: A Critique." *Freshman English News* 13 (1984): 16-18.

Collins, A. *Learning to Read and Write with Computers* (Reading Education Report No. 42). Washington, D.C.: National Institute of Education, 1983.

Corbett, E.P.J. *Classical Rhetoric for the Modern Student.* New York: Oxford University Press, 1971.

Daiute, C.A. "Psycholinguistic Perspectives on Revising." In *Revising: New Essays for Teachers of Writing.* Edited by R.A. Sudol. Urbana, Ill.: National Council of Teachers of Writing, 1982.

de Beaugrande, R. *Text Production: Toward a Science of Composition.* Norwood, N.J.: Ablex, 1984.

de Bono, E. *CoRT 1: Teachers Notes.* New York: Pergamon, 1973.

Elbow, P. *Writing Without Teachers.* New York: Oxford University Press, 1975.

Elbow, P. *Writing With Power: Techniques for Mastering the Writing Process.* New York: Oxford University Press, 1981.

Flower, L.S. *Problem-Solving Strategies for Writing.* New York: Harcourt, Brace, Jovanovich, 1981.

Flower, L.S., and Hayes, J.R. "A Cognitive Process Theory of Writing." Paper presented at the meeting of the Conference on College Composition and Communication, Washington, D.C., 1980.

Fulwiler, T. "Journal Writing Across the Curriculum." Paper presented at the meeting of the Conference on College Composition and Communication, Denver, March 1978.

Gelman, R., and Baillargeon, R. "A Review of Some Piagetian Concepts." In *Handbook of Child Psychology* (Vol. 3). Edited by J. Flavell and E. M. Markman. New York: Wiley, 1983.

Giroux, H.A. "Teaching Content and Thinking Through Writing." *Social Education* 43 (1979): 190-193.

Glatthorn, A.A. *Writing in the Schools: Improvement Through Effective Leadership.* Reston, Va.: National Association of Secondary School Principals, 1981.

Glatthorn, A.A. *Differentiated Supervision.* Alexandria, Va.: Association for Supervision and Curriculum Development, 1984.

Glatthorn, A.A. "Modeling the Good Student Thinker." Philadelphia: University of Pennsylvania, 1984.

Hillocks, G. "The Effects of Observational Activities on Student Writing." *Research in the Teaching of English* 13 (1979): 23-35.

Humes, A. "Research on the Composing Process." *Review of Educational Research* 53 (1983): 201-216.

Irmscher, W. *Holt Guide to English.* New York: Holt, Rinehart, and Winston, 1972.

Johannessen, L.R.; Kahn, E.A.; and Walter, CC. *Designing and Sequencing Prewriting Activities.* Urbana, Ill.: National Council of Teachers of English, 1982.

Kroll, B.M. "A Cognitive-Developmental Approach to the Teaching of Composition." Paper presented at the annual meeting of the Midwest Regional Conference on English in Two-Year Colleges, Des Moines, February 1979.

Kroll, B.M., and Shaefer, J.C. "The Development of Error Analysis and Its Implications for the Teaching of Composition." Paper presented at the meeting of the Conference on College Composition and Communication, Kansas City, Missouri, March 1977.

Larson, R.L. "The Writer's Mind: Recent Research and Unanswered Questions." In *The Writer's Mind: Writing as a Mode of Thinking.* Edited by J.N. Hays, P.A. Roth, J.R. Ramsey, and R.D. Foulke. Urbana, Ill.: National Council of Teachers of English, 1983.

Lipman, M.L. "Philosophy and the Cultivation of Reasoning." Symposium conducted by the Association for Supervision and Curriculum Development, Racine, Wisconsin, May 1984.

Nickerson, R.S. "Teaching Thinking: What is Being Done and With What Results?" Symposium conducted by the Association for Supervision and Curriculum Development, Racine, Wisconsin, May 1984.

Odell, L. "Piaget, Problem-Solving, and Freshman Composition." *College Composition and Communication* 24 (1973): 36-42.

Odell, L. "Written Products and the Writing Process." In *The Writer's Mind: Writing as a Mode of Thinking.* Edited by J.N. Hays, P.A. Roth, J.R. Ramsey, and R.D. Foulke, Urbana, Ill.: National Council of Teachers of English, 1983.

Parnes, S.J.; Noller, R.B.; and Biondi, A.M. *Guide to Creative Action.* New York: Scribner's, 1977.

Perron, J.D. "Written Syntactic Complexity and the Modes of Discourse." Paper presented at the annual meeting of the American Educational Research Association, New York, April 1977.

Piaget, J. *The Origins of Intelligence in Children.* New York: International Universities Press, 1952.

Polanyi, M. *The Tacit Dimension.* New York: Doubleday, 1966.

Rohman, D.G. "Pre-Writing: The Stage of Discovery in the Writing Process." *College Composition and Communication* 16 (1965): 106-112.

Scardamalia, M. "How Children Cope with the Cognitive Demands of Writing." In *Writing: Nature, Development, and Teaching of Written Communication* (Vol. 2). Edited by C.H. Frederiksen and J.F. Dominic. Hillsdale, N.J.: Earlbaum, 1981.

Scardamalia, M.; Bereiter, C.; and McDonald, J.D.S. "Role Taking in Written Communication Investigated by Manipulating Anticipatory Knowledge." Paper presented at the biennial meeting of the Society for Research in Child Development, New Orleans, March 1977.

Shaughnessy, M. *Errors and Expectations.* New York: Oxford University Press, 1977.

Sigel, I.E. "Reflection on Thinking About Thinking: The Educational Discovery of the 80s?" Symposium conducted by the Association for Supervision and Curriculum Development, Racine, Wisconsin, May 1984.

Sternberg, R.J. *How Can We Teach Intelligence?* Philadelphia: Research for Better Schools, 1983.

Sudol, R.A., ed. *Revising: New Strategies for Teachers of Writing.* Urbana, Ill.: National Council of Teachers of English, 1982.

Vygotsky, L.S. *Mind in Society: The Development of Higher Psychological Processes.* Cambridge: Harvard University Press, 1978.

Wales, C.E., and Stager, R.A. *Guided Design.* Morgantown, W.Va.: West Virginia University, 1977.

Weiss, R.H. "Writing to Learn." Paper presented at the meeting of the American Educational Research Association, Boston, April 1980.

Whimbey, A., and Lochhead, J. *Problem Solving and Comprehension: A Short Course in Analytical Reasoning.* 2nd ed. Philadelphia: Franklin Institute, 1981.

Witte, S., and Faigley, L. "Analyzing Revision." *College Composition and Communication* 32 (1981): 400-407.

Wotring, A.M. "Writing to Think About High School Chemistry." Master's thesis, George Mason University, Fairfax, Virginia, 1980.

Yinger, R.J., and Clark, C.M. *Reflective Journal Writing: Theory and Practice.* East Lansing, Mich.: Institute for Research on Teaching, 1981.

Young, R.; Becker, A.; and Pike, D. *Rhetoric: Discovery and Change.* New York: Harcourt, Brace, Jovanovich, 1970.

5. Instrumental Enrichment: A Strategy for Cognitive and Academic Improvement

Frances R. Link

WHAT LIES BEHIND A STUDENT'S FAILURE TO THINK? ALL TOO OFTEN WE attribute an inability to perform a given operation to a lack of knowledge of the principles involved, or worse, to a low intelligence that precludes the student's understanding of those principles. What is overlooked is that the specific deficiency may reside not in the operational level or specific content of the child's thought processes but in the underlying functions upon which successful thinking depends.

This distinction is crucial to any valuable understanding of a student's corrective needs, which should take into account not only what they cannot do but why they cannot do it. Consider for a moment a problem requiring the mental classification of objects or events. Its solution necessarily involves subordinate mental functions such as systematic and precise data gathering, the ability to deal with two or more sources of information simultaneously, and the comparison of objects or events to be classified. A student incapable of performing and applying these prerequisite operations can hardly be expected to perform the overall task. Clearly, if teachers fail to identify the specific source of the child's cognitive weakness, corrective actions in this area will suffer.

Improving the overall cognitive performance of the low-achieving adolescent demands a broad-scale strategy of intervention whose focus is not any specific skills or subject but, is rather, the process of learning itself. Instrumental Enrichment is such a program: a direct and focused attack on mental processes that, through their absence, their fragility, or their inefficiency, are to blame for poor intellectual or academic performance.

The core of the Instrumental Enrichment Program—developed by Reuven Feuerstein, an Israeli clinical psychologist—is a three-year series of problem-solving tasks and exercises that are grouped in 14 areas of specific cognitive development. They are called instruments rather than lessons because in and of themselves they are virtually free of specific subject matter. Their purpose is to serve as the means or vehicle for cognition-oriented interactions between teacher and students. Each instrument's true goal is not the learner's acquisition of information but the development, refinement, and crystallization of functions that are prerequisite to effective thinking (see Figure 5.1). In terms of behavior, Instrumental Enrichment's ultimate aims is to transform retarded performers by altering their characteristically passive and dependent cognitive style so that they become more active, self-motivated, independent thinkers.

There are six major goals of Instrumental Enrichment:

1. To correct weaknesses and deficiencies in cognitive functions.

2. To help students learn and apply the basic concepts, labels, vocabulary, and operations essential to effective thought.

3. To produce sound and spontaneous thinking habits leading to greater curiosity, self-confidence, and motivation.

4. To produce in students increasingly reflective and insightful thought processes.

5. To motivate students toward task-oriented abstract goals rather than toward objectives of impulsive self-gratification.

6. To transform poor learners from passive recipients and reproducers of information into active generators of new information.

Figure 5.1. Instrumental Enrichment Cognitive Functions

I. Gathering all the information we need (input)

1. Using our senses (listening, seeing, smelling, tasting, touching, feeling) to gather clear and complete information (clear perception).
2. Using a system or plan so that we do not skip or miss something important or repeat ourselves (systematic exploration).
3. Giving the thing we gather through our senses and our experience a name so that we can remember it more clearly and talk about it (labeling).
4. Describing things and events in terms of where and when they occur (temporal and spatial referents).
5. Deciding on the characteristics of a thing or event that always stays the same, even when changes take place (conservation, constancy, and object permanence).
6. Organizing the information we gather by considering more than one thing at a time (using two sources of information).
7. Being precise and accurate when it matters (need for precision).

II. Using the information we have gathered (elaboration)

1. Defining what the problem is, what we are being asked to do, and what we must figure out (analyzing disequilibrium).
2. Using only that part of the information we have gathered that is relevant, that is, that applies to the problem and ignoring the rest (relevance).
3. Having a good picture in our mind of what we are looking for or what we must do (interiorization).
4. Making a plan that will include the steps we need to take to reach our goal (planning behavior).
5. Remembering and keeping in mind the various pieces of information we need (broadening our mental field).
6. Looking for the relationship by which separate objects, events, and experiences can be tied together (projecting relationships).
7. Comparing objects and experiences to others to see what is similar and what is different (comparative behavior).
8. Finding the class or set to which the new object or experience belongs (categorization).
9. Thinking about different possibilities and figuring out what would happen if we were to choose one or another (hypothetical thinking).
10. Using logic to prove things and to defend our opinion (locigal evidence).

III. Expressing the solution to a problem (output)

1. Being clear and precise in our language to be sure that there is no question as to what the answer is. Putting ourselves into the "shoes" of the listener to be sure that our answers will be understood (overcoming egocentric communication).
2. Thinking things through before we answer instead of immediately trying to answer and making a mistake, and then trying again (overcoming trial-and-error).
3. Counting to ten (at least) so that we do not say or do something we will be sorry for later (restraining impulsive behavior).
4. Not fretting or panicking if for some reason we cannot answer a question even though we "know" the answer. Leaving the question for a little while and then, when we return to it, using a strategy to help us find the answer (overcoming blocking).

Why do Students Fail?

Numerous causes have been suggested to explain poor cognitive performance, ranging from heredity to environment. At one extreme, Jensen (1969, 1973) held that mental ability is largely determined by genetics and thus is inaccessible to substantial modification. He proposed a dichotomous model of intelligence in which humanity is divided according to genetic endowment: people whose capacities are limited to simple mental acts of an associative and reproductive nature and people able to use complex transformational, operational, and abstract processes. Jensen suggests we accept the limits imposed by heredity and adjust educational goals downward for those with low intelligence. This is the position of defeat.

At the opposite extreme, we encounter the notion or fantasy that the retarded performer's failure can be traced to unreasonable demands imposed by an insensitive and alien school system. This theory, the "cultural difference" position, implies that merely altering the student's learning environment will produce the desired changes and will eliminate poor performance. This gross oversimplification fails to recognize that deficient cognitive functioning is neither culture bound nor limited to the classroom, occurring as it does in many different situations. A student may master education's "three Rs" yet still be incapable of adapting to new information, demands, and responsibilities both in school and later in life, for lack of the fourth R: Reasoning.

Between these opposite points of view lie a host of intermediate theories, all of which share the belief, either implicit or explicit, that the persistence of poor cognitive performance beyond childhood is a condition beyond remedy. All are, fundamentally, at variance with the goals and strategies of Feuerstein's Instrumental Enrichment (Feuerstein, 1980).

Retarded Performance: A Temporary State

In contrast, Instrumental Enrichment is firmly rooted in the concept of cognitive modifiability as the working channel for improving the underlying processes of thought. The program's essential aim is not merely remediation of specific behaviors but basic structural changes that alter the individual's whole course of cognitive development.

One common misconception to be overcome is that retarded performance is an irreversible state. The term *retardation* has, unfortunately, come to imply that an individual's capacity for development is fixed. Yet evidence is mounting that, except for the most severe cases of organic impairment, the human mind is open to modification at all ages and stages of development. The term *retarded performance*, therefore, is meant to stress that what is retarded is no more than the individual's manifest cognitive ability at the time. It is not a label for any supposedly stable and immutable characteristic of the individual's ultimate potential.

Although it is a pervasive state, retarded performance is neither permanent nor irreversible. Retarded performers do not make connections based on former experiences in learning. They do not spontaneously build relationships. They view the world and learning in an episodic manner. They do not seem to learn from direct exposure to experience. By changing the cognitive structure rather than selected dimensions of behavior, we can achieve a permanent, stable state of capacity for improvement.

Cognitive Modifiability: To Adapt, To Survive

To understand what is meant by cognitive modifiability and why it is such a valuable human attribute, one must appreciate the difference between structural changes in cognitive development and other kinds of developmental processes. In the normal course of events, a child undergoes a series of changes. These may be of a maturational nature, such as the transition from crawling to walking, or they may result from exposure to specific sets of circumstances, such as learning a particular arithmetic operation or a foreign language.

Unlike development spurred by random experiences, structural changes reflect a person's entire manner of dealing with and responding to information and stimulation. Modifying this cognitive structure demands a particular kind of mediation or intervention by the parent or teacher, which renders individuals receptive and sensitive to sources of information and stimulation from which they would otherwise be incapable of benefiting.

Cognitive modification promotes continuous growth by opening the channels for adapting to the demands of life and of the environment. The survival of any organism depends on its ability to respond, not to a stable environment but to situations and circumstances continually in flux. Ultimately, the Instrumental Enrichment curriculum attempts to provide learners with the means for their survival in school and throughout life.

The Mind as a Container: Open or Closed

Instrumental Enrichment's active modification approach contrasts sharply with the passive acceptance approach, which attempts to adjust external conditions to suit the limited abilities currently manifested by retarded performers. A case in point is special education. Not only the modes of training but also its goals are based on so-called "realistic limits" indicated by current levels of functioning. Special education deems the child's cognitive structure an immutable entity and keeps attempts to elicit change within this presumed capacity. This approach sees the mind as a rigid container with predetermined limits to what it may contain. It does not view the mind as the dynamic, flexible system with a capacity and structure that can change through adolescence and beyond, as learners' latent functions interact with new stimulation.

At the heart of the matter lies the issue of whether the mind is an open or closed system. When intelligence is conceptualized in quantitative terms as a fixed product of ability that is constant through life, passive acceptance of the present condition is the outcome. Attempts to modify an individual's course of development come to be regarded as futile, even unfair, because they demand the "impossible."

The common response is to confirm the observed low level of performance using tests specifically designed to measure such performance. Students' low achievement in school is confirmed by poor performance on tests. After testing, students are classified, labeled, and left at their current stage of functioning. This exercise in the self-fulfilling prophecy, needless to say, holds devastating implications for the ultimate destiny of students.

The Instruments: What They Do

The instruments provide sufficient material for one-period lessons given two to five days a week. Although a three-year sequence is recommended, the program may be implemented in two years, depending on the class curriculum and students' needs. Instrumental Enrichment is not intended to replace traditional content areas but is intended as a supplement to help students get the most out of all opportunities to learn and grow. It is a form of general intervention enabling the teacher and students to make *bridges* to both specific and general subject areas. The Instruments are tools for learning to learn. The goal is the development of higher mental processes, not minimum competencies.

First Year Curriculum

Organization of Dots. The aim of this initial instrument is to produce in the student the spontaneous ability to discern relations among data that may not be clearly organized. Students find the relations—shapes, figures, and other attributes—among a field of dots, much the way one picks out constellations in the night sky. In this way students begin developing strategies for linking perceived events into a system yielding comprehensible information that can be a basis for understanding and logical response. Perceptual problems, spatial, planning, and organizational abilities are mediated by use of this instrument.

Orientation in Space I. This instrument promotes the creation of specific strategies for differentiating frames of reference in space, particularly with regard to the student's personal frame of reference. Left, right, front, and back are the major concepts developed. This instrument also helps illuminate the important differences between systems based on relative measures or quantities as opposed to those dealing in absolutes, and demonstrates how strategies for dealing with each must adjust accordingly. The development of "point of view" in personal, political, literary, and social relationships is the focus of bridging activities.

Comparisons. The spontaneous and efficient comparison of behaviors, ideas, and events is an ability crucial to continuous cognitive development. This instrument, therefore, fosters precise perception, the ability to discriminate by attribute (equal/unequal, similar/dissimilar), and the judgment necessary to identify and evaluate similarities and differences.

Analytic Perception. This instrument addresses the ability to analyze component parts in order to find how they relate to each other as well as how they contribute to the overall character of the whole they compose. Students learn to recognize how systematic analytical processes may be applied in a variety of ways to physical structure, to the different parts of an activity or operation, to the reasons through which an act is explained, and to the creation of logical propositions.

Second Year Curriculum

Categorization. In this instrument, students learn not simply how to sort objects or events, but the underlying principles and strategies for creating conceptual sets and categories, a vital prerequisite for higher mental processing. By finding the common attributes that go into the formation of categories, students develop the abilities to perceive, label, and compare, as well as to differentiate between relevant and irrelevant information.

Instructions. Instructions emphasize the use of language as a system for both encoding and decoding operational processes on levels of varying complexity. By requiring students to read and carry out directions precisely, it promotes systematic, ordered thought and response. Exercises also focus on critiquing instruction, rewriting instructions to supply missing relevant data, and creating instructions for others to follow.

Temporal Relations. This instrument addresses chronological time, biological time, and other temporal relations. Students learn to isolate the factors involved in evaluating or predicting outcomes—time, distance, velocity—and to find the interrelation among those factors. Problems force students to seek all relevant information, such as starting points, routes, distances, and terrain, before attempting to compare and summarize, thus restraining impulsiveness and stressing the need for planning.

Numerical Progressions. This instrument promotes the ability to perceive and understand principles and formulas manifested in numerical patterns. By searching for the principles involved in ascending and descending numerical progressions, students learn to establish relations among events and to discover the rhythms by which relations repeat themselves.

Family Relationships. Although the title of this instrument suggests the study of relationships among kin, its larger goal is the promotion of a clearer understanding of how individual roles in hierarchical organizations define the network of relationships that are encountered in daily life and work. In short, Family Relations helps bring into focus the complexity of relationships within the human family and in all hierarchical structures.

Illustrations. This is a collection of situational cartoons that present, in graphic form, problems students must perceive, recognize, and interpret. Its aim is to encourage a spontaneous awareness that a problem exists, an analysis of why it exists, and a projection of cause-and-effect relations. Unlike other instruments, Illustrations need not be taught sequentially but can be interspersed among other instruments as needed to assess mastery or correct specific operations.

Third Year Curriculum

Transitive Relations and Syllogisms. These two instruments, usually taught together, foster the higher level abstract and inferential thought for which the student has been prepared by mastery of earlier instruments. Transitive Relations deals with drawing inferences from relations that can be described in terms of "greater than," "equal to," or "less than." In effect, the student learns the rules governing transitive thinking and learns to connect separately presented statements by means of a common reference point. Syllogisms deals with formal propositional logic and aims at promoting inferential thinking based on local evidence. Students learn the laws governing sets and their members as well as how to construct new sets by such operations as logical multiplication. In addition to learning formal syllogistic thought, students learn to critique analytic premises and propositions.

Representational Stencil Design. One of the most advanced instruments in the program, Representational Stencil Design calls into play a broad range of higher level thought processes addressed in previous instruments. Completing its tasks requires an intricate series of steps: analyzing a complex figure, identifying its components, and recreating the whole mentally in color, shape, size, and orientation.

Orientation in Space III. This final instrument deals with spatial relations according to standard conventions: north, east, south, and west. It complements the earlier instrument in spatial orientation by extending students' understanding of relative positions from a personal orientation to the stable external system represented by the points of the compass. Personal and external orientations are integrated in a way that permits students to use both simultaneously.

The Means: Mediated Learning Experience

The development of higher mental processes cannot be understood without the powerful adjunct concept of mediated learning experience. This refers to a particular kind of experience, which, for all its technical-sounding name, is a familiar and integral part of growing up for most of us.

In its earlier manifestations, mediated learning experience is the way parents and later teachers instruct children and transmit cultural elements. Guided by intentions, culture, and emotional investment, "mediating" agents select and organize children's world of stimuli toward a particular goal of behavior and attitude. As a result of such mediation, children acquire the learning sets and operating structures for mentally organizing, processing, and acting on information gathered from internal and external sources.

Mediated learning experience may be viewed as the means by which nascent, elementary cognitive sets and habits are transformed into the bases for effective thinking. Consequently, the earlier and the more often children are subjected to mediated learning experience, the greater will be their capacity to efficiently perceive, understand, and respond to information and stimulation in and out of school. The less mediation children experience both in quantity and quality, the less prepared they will be for school and for life.

If this concept is accepted, one can readily see that evidence is accumulating for Instrumental Enrichment as a substitute for early mediated learning experience. By interposing the Instrumental Enrichment program, the teacher can facilitate the organization and transmission of information at increasingly complex, abstract, and efficient levels of functioning. Mediated learning experience of this kind hastens the development of the prerequisite cognitive structures that enable a human being to learn and grow. At stake is not merely the acquisition of particular skills or abilities but the opportunity to radically divert the adolescent's stubborn course of failure and to institute a pattern of growth and development. In summary, Feuerstein's concept of mediation and intelligence lies not in its measured product but rather in its active construction.

Teacher Training in Instrumental Enrichment

Whatever the particular focus of an instrument, its larger purpose is always the further development of students' conscious thought processes and their discovery of practical applications and transfer of those processes in and out of school. In this effort, teachers play the crucial role as mediating agents.

To perform this role, teachers require special training in Instrumental Enrichment's basic precepts, materials, and teaching strategies. They must learn how to extract the thinking processes and principles from an instrument and how to help students learn to "bridge" or apply them. Teachers, moreover, must focus the educational experience set in motion by the exercises to help students understand in cognitive or problem-solving terms what their performance means. This focusing will help students overcome the frustration and alienation engendered by past failures to learn or limited opportunity to think on higher cognitive levels.

The teacher as a *human* mediator learns to apply the important aspects of Mediated Learning Experience (MEL), which include:

Intentionality of meaning
Transcendence ·
Mediation of meaning
Mediation of feeling of competence

Mediated sharing behavior
Mediated regulation and control of behavior
Mediated individuation and psychological differentiation
Mediation of goal seeking, goal setting, and goal-achieving planning behavior
Mediation of challenge: the search for novelty and complexity.

Teacher training thus involves a minimum of 45 hours of inservice annually, plus on-the-job use of exercises in the classroom, if possible, while training is in process. Training programs are custom designed to fit the inservice schedules of school systems.

Teacher training concentrates on the following three areas:

1. Understanding and accepting Instrumental Enrichment's fundamental theories and concepts.

2. Mastery in the classroom use of the instruments by learning to plan lessons that focus on the six subgoals of Instrumental Enrichment.

3. Special techniques for mediating, bridging, developing insight, and applying cognitive processes to specific subject matter and to life experiences.

Many school systems have been conducting evaluation studies. The three reported in this chapter demonstrate the variety of methods of evaluation. The changes in self-image, motivation, and intellectual growth across a variety of populations, and the improvement in teaching, seem to be consistent results in all the studies.

Cognitive Modification for the Hearing-Impaired Adolescent: The Promise

A pilot study of the effects of the cognitive intervention program Instrumental Enrichment for hearing-impaired adolescents was conducted at the Model Secondary School for the Deaf in Washington, D.C. (see Martin, 1984). Experimental and control groups were contrasted in regard to general cognitive functioning, problem-solving strategies, and reading comprehension. Experimental subjects demonstrated improvements in the following areas: (1) systematic approaches to problems, (2) analysis of problem situations, (3) vocabulary size, (4) analysis of source of error in problem-solving situations, (5) completeness, organization, and planning in problem-solving situations, (6) peer cooperation in problem solving, (7) abstract thinking, (8) precision, and (9) development of multiple strategies to solve a problem. These results establish the efficacy and strong potential of systematic cognitive intervention programs for improvement of thinking skills in the hearing-impaired adolescent.

At the end of the second pilot year, hearing-impaired students who had systematic experiences in "cognitive education" (a) showed consistent improvement in problem-solving interviews in regard to the practicality, completeness, organization, and systematic planning of their problem solutions; (b) significantly improved their nonverbal logical thinking as shown on the *Raven's Matrices;* (c) more frequently expected themselves to be precise, were able to describe several strategies to solve a problem, and defended their opinions on the basis of logical evidence, as shown by teacher observation checklists; (d) demonstrated important gains in reading comprehension; and (e) demonstrated important gains in mathematical computation.

In regard to the cognitive problems of the hearing-impaired cited in the review of the literature, these data indicate that this intervention holds promise for the improvement of spatial reasoning skills (Parasnis and Long, 1979), the ability to consider two or more sources of information simultaneously (Ottem, 1980), the ability to carry out analogical reasoning (Meadow, 1980), the ability to develop the concept of comparison and opposition (Furth, 1964; Meadow, 1980), and the ability to understand cause-and-effect relations (Johnson, 1981). To the degree that memory is involved with the reading comprehension and mathematics computation subtests of the SAT-HI, it indicates that the problem cited by Karchmer and Belmont (1976) is amenable to improvement. In addition, the emphasis on meta-cognition activities during Instrumental Enrichment lessons must be considered as at least one factor in the improvement of experimental students; this interpretation should corroborate the finding elsewhere (Peterson, Swing, Stark, and Waas, 1983) that students who can explain why they understood a cognitive task tend to have higher achievement scores.

From these results, the following recommendations emerge for future efforts in cognitive education of hearing-impaired adolescents:

1. Systematic (as opposed to incidental) cognitive intervention is important in the context of the ongoing school curriculum.

2. Adolescence is apparently not "too late" in the development of a hearing-impaired learner to make important and measurable modifications in cognitive functioning.

3. In-depth teacher training in cognitive education is an essential prerequisite to the success of any cognitive intervention program with students.

4. Future studies should investigate in depth the apparently positive perceptions of teachers who are engaged in cognitive education—

just why are they so enthusiastic?

5. Larger student samples and more complex evaluation designs are needed to assess in more depth the statistical effects of this intervention for hearing-impaired adolescents. Included in such studies should also be an investigation of possible aptitude–treatment interactions.

The continuing high enthusiasm of the original pilot teachers has led to the involvement of a total of 39 teachers at the school in cognitive education for 1984–85—a sign of strong professional commitement to the idea that positive growth is occurring in the problem-solving skills of the students in this population. Such professional commitment and enthusiasm may be the most important indicators of all.

New York City Special Projects Evaluation Report[1]

This study of regular education students who qualified for remedial instruction was conducted in New York City. In the fall of 1980, the Instrumental Enrichment Program (IE) trained eight teachers in the nonpublic school Chapter I program.[2] Instrumental Enrichment classes began in November of 1980 with 134 students. In September of 1981, 135 students were in the program; 96 were second-year students. In the fall of 1982, 203 students were participating; 65 were third-year students and 14 were second-year students. The evaluation found after the second year that students made achievement gains ranging from 2.2 to 8.0 normal curve equivalents.

Although the program served more students in 1982–83, the same eight teachers who were initially trained continued with the program. Each teacher taught IE to as many as three groups of eight to ten students two or three times a week in 45-minute or 60-minute sessions.

Based on severity of need, Chapter I-eligible students were placed in Chapter I remedial reading or mathematics pull-out groups. From the groups that met five times a week, 21 classes were designated to receive IE instruction two or three times a week. The 21 classes se-

---

[1]Project Director: Larry Larkin, New York City Special Projects Division.

[2]Nonpublic schools were selected if they were providing Chapter I corrective reading, reading skills, or mathematics at least five times per week in grades 4 to 7 and if teachers had at least two years of experience in Chapter I. Chapter I services were provided by public school teachers under the supervision of the Office of Special Projects, Bureau of Nonpublic School Reimbursable Services.

lected included students who were continuing in the program and students whose remediation needs were greater.

The major objectives of the nonpublic school IE Program are listed below:

1. The reading achievement of IE students will be greater than that of a group of non-IE students, as measured by the reading comprehension subtest of the California Achievement Test (CAT).

2. The mathematics achievement of IE students will improve as measured by the applications subtest and the total mathematics score on the Stanford Achievement Test (SAT).[3]

3. Students in the IE program will develop positive attitudes about their participation in IE.

4. The IE Program will be implemented as designed by program developers.

Evaluation Methodology

The 1982–83 evaluation of the IE Program was guided by three questions, derived from the program's objectives.

1. To what extent did students improve their reading and mathematics skills? How do the reading scores of IE students compare with randomly selected non-IE, nonpublic school students receiving remedial reading or mathematics services?

2. To what extent do students have positive attitudes towards the IE Program?

3. Was the program implemented according to the training received? What were teachers' attitudes towards the availability, comprehensibility, and continued use of IE materials?

Conclusions and Recommendations

The Instrumental Enrichment Program has been successful in terms of student achievement, students' perceptions, and teachers' perceptions. IE students made substantial gains, which were greater than those of non-IE students. Responses to the student questionnaire were highly positive, and teachers were unanimous in their enthusiasm for the program.

Observations of IE classes gave evidence that teachers adhered to the program design. The overall dynamics in the classroom in terms of activities, interactions, and the students' display of skills were con-

---

[3]Because the number of mathematics students in IE in each grade level was small, no comparisons were made with a non-IE group.

sistent with the program design. This close match between what teachers should be doing and what was observed was one source of the program's success in the Nonpublic School Chapter I classes. The teachers were able to execute the program successfully due to the intensive teacher training they received during the first year and the support they continually receive from the program's administrators.

Another source of the program's success was the motivation it provided for students to achieve. Teachers said students have a chance to state their opinions, right or wrong. This helps them understand how to live with errors, and, consequently, they are not afraid of making mistakes. Other behaviors observed by the teachers that contributed to the students' success were less impulsivity, more task-orientation, higher tolerance for frustration, a sense of accomplishment, and increased self-esteem and confidence.

The third source of the IE Program's success is summarized in the comment of one IE teacher, "I expect more of the students, more thinking, and I see them as more capable of handling any task." It is well known in the educational community that when a teacher has this kind of positive attitude toward the students, the students will perform better than they would with a teacher who has lower expectations.

"Making Up Our Minds"

In the United Kingdom, a case study approach (Making Up Our Minds; Craft and Weller, 1983) was designed with a wide variety of age groups and populations. In 1980 the Organization for Economic Cooperation and Development (OECD), the then Schools Council, and five Local Education Authorities (LEA) agreed to mount a two-year study of Instrumental Enrichment in United Kingdom schools. Each LEA selected two to four institutions to take part in the study.

Instrumental Enrichment was taught in 17 establishments in inner London, Somerset, Coventry, Manchester, and Sheffield Education Authorities. One college of further education was involved, together with an equal number of special schools and comprehensive high schools.

Local evaluators from universities were asked to visit each class at least once every term and to submit a record of observations to the Schools Council. Evaluators and LEA coordinators also wrote short progress reports early in 1982 and kept records of discussions. A cumulative record of experience, therefore, has been available to Schools Council coordinators, and it provides the basis of this interim review.

Institutions organized IE teaching in a wide range of different ways. Some offered short intensive courses; others employed extended light programs. In consequence, pupils' weekly contact time with IE varied widely. Some teachers worked alone, whereas others benefited from ancillary help and team-teaching techniques. Often, particularly in the special schools, teachers taught IE to classes with whom they spent a large part of the week. Pupils receiving IE teaching were mainly between 11 to 15 years of age; most were retarded performers, and some had behavior problems.

There was a strong general impression that pupils, including retarded performers, were benefiting from IE. The evidence was mixed but was largely positive—in some cases extremely so. Evaluators' observations have frequently shown that pupils enjoy lessons—they are interested, motivated, and increasing in self-confidence. Pupils were felt to be learning in most lessons observed. One evaluator remarked on the apparent ability of even seriously handicapped pupils to keep up with the group. In some cases, teachers reported improvements in attendance and behavior and noted increases in pupils' spans of concentration.

Some teachers reported improvements by IE pupils in other subjects and commented on better attitudes and study skills. Others noted increased concern for accuracy and planning; pupils were described as less impulsive and as concerned with checking work more carefully. In two schools, pupils joined examination courses as a result of improvements attributed to IE. Of course, one must recognize that the stimulus and extra attention associated with innovation is always likely to produce positive results, but evidence now accruing suggests that momentum is being maintained and gains are lasting.

Teachers have inevitably needed time to gain confidence with the new materials and teaching strategies. Some are still working on handling discussions and relating work covered in IE to other subjects and contexts ("bridging").

However, there is evidence that the materials have had a significant effect on teachers. Many are spending much time preparing IE lessons and, in consequence, are thinking harder about their teaching strategies. Many also say they have revised upwards their expectations of pupils. In the words of one teacher:

A number of children have shown insights, used language or solved problems that I would previously have thought unlikely.

In summary, it can be said that Instrumental Enrichment has been generally well received by teachers and pupils in the United

Kingdom. The work has not been without its problems, but many of these have organizational roots that would apply to any curriculum innovation. A closing comment from an evaluator may give something of the flavor of the work:

The children were consciously thinking problems through . . . the teacher wondered whether working with the materials had alerted her to the nature of problems and changed the way she taught.

As a result of this study, in 1985, throughout the United Kingdom, 25 local Education Authorities have trained teachers to implement Instrumental Enrichment.

Instrumental Enrichment in Schaumburg, Illinois

The following is from the August 1985 report of School District 54 in Schaumburg, Illinois.

INTRODUCTION

Instrumental Enrichment (IE) is an instructional program intended to improve thinking skills. The developers of IE collected reports from school districts that have used the program. These reports indicate that the use of the IE program improves thinking skills and achievement. The reports also indicate that the significance of IE's impact on achievement depends upon a consistent schedule of instruction in IE—90 to 120 minutes a week over a two-year period.

This evaluation of our district's implementation of the IE program focuses specifically upon a group of students who received IE instruction during 5th and 6th grades and its impact upon their measurable thinking skills. These students needed to be pre- and post-tested before they were dispersed at various junior high schools. The achievement scores of the IE students will be included in next year's evaluation of the IE program—after the Fall 1985 CAT/C testing has taken place.

PROCEDURE

In Fall 1983 some 5th grade teachers in almost every school were trained and began implementing the IE programs. For the following year these students continued with the program in their 6th grade classes. *Cognitive Abilities Test* data were obtained on these students in Fall 1983 and again in Spring 1985. These data represent the pre-test and post-test information respectively. The final group whose test scores are used in this evaluation included only those students who studied IE for two consecutive years—grades 5 and 6. There were 428 such students.

RESULTS

1. The evaluation group's average "Verbal," "Quantitative," and "Non-Verbal" subtest scores on *Cognitive Abilities Test* were higher on the post-test than on the pre-test.

2. The increase from pre-test to post-test in the "Quantitative" and "Non-Verbal" subtest average scores was statistically significant (at the .05 level).

Discussion

The data from the current two-year study of the IE program are consistent with the data obtained from our previous study of the IE program, which was conducted in our junior high schools' Immature Student Program. They also used material from the IE Program as a part of their curriculum. In both instances the data confirm that the consistent use of the IE program does increase measurable thinking skills in students.

References

Craft, Alma, and Weller, Keith. *Making Up Our Minds: An Exploratory Study of Instrumental Enrichment.* London: Schools Council Publications, 1983.

Feuerstein, R. *Instrumental Enrichment.* Baltimore: University Park Press, 1980.

Furth, H. *Thinking Without Language.* New York: Free Press, 1963.

Jackson, Yvette F. "Identification of Potential Giftedness in Disadvantaged Students." Doctoral dissertation, Columbia University, Teachers College, 1983.

Jensen, A.R. "How Much Can We Boost IQ and Scholastic Achievement?" *Harvard Educational Review* 39 (1969): 1-123.

Jensen, A.R. *Educability and Group Differences.* London: Methuen, 1973.

Johnson, J. "Hearing-Impaired Learner with Special Needs." Symposium, Lincoln, Nebraska, April 1981.

Karchmer, M.A., and Belmont, J.M. "On Assessing and Improving Deaf Performance in the Cognitive Laboratory." Report presented at the meeting of the American Speech and Hearing Association, Houston, Texas, November 1976.

Martin, David. "Cognitive Modification for the Hearing Impaired Adolescent: The Promise." *Deafness and Child Development.* Berkeley: University of California Press, 1980.

Ottem, E. "An Analysis of Cognitive Studies with Deaf Subjects." *American Annals of the Deaf* 125, 5 (1980): 564-575.

Parasnis, I., and Long, G.L. "Relationships Among Spatial Skills, Communication Skills, and Field Dependence in Deaf Students." *Directions* 1, 2 (1979): 26-37.

Peterson, P.L.; Swing, S.R.; Stark, K.D.; and Waas, G.A. "Students' Reports of Their Cognitive Processes During Classroom Instruction." Research report from the University of Wisconsin presented at the Conference of the American Educational Research Association, Montreal, March 1977.

6. Development of Intellectual Capability

Elliott Jaques

IN THIS CHAPTER WE ARE CONCERNED WITH THE ABILITY OF INDIVIDUALS to engage in goal-directed behavior in problem solving and in everyday work—that is, intellectual capability or what is currently referred to as cognitive processes. Cognitive processes are the ways in which individuals form or pattern the world they construct and work with. There are several issues involved. What is the nature of cognitive processes? How is it possible to measure the scale or degree of complexity of cognitive processes—defined here as cognitive power? And what is the pattern of development of an individual's cognitive power; how does it mature and grow?

Cognitive power is, of course, not the only component of the competencies required in work. A person must also possess the psychological tools and outlook—the knowledge, experience, skill, temperament, character, and values—required by particular types of work. But cognitive power is of special importance when it comes to assessing the *level* of work, or responsibility, that a person might be capable of carrying.

The stratified systems theory uses a temporal scale to measure

Author's Note: The development of the ideas in this chapter has been supported by Grant No. DAJA37-80-C-007 from the U.S. Army Research Institute for the Behavioral and Social Sciences.

cognitive power and posits that human cognitive functions are discontinuous, or distributed multimodally, rather than being distributed continuously or unimodally. It has, of course, been well established since the work of Piaget that intellectual or cognitive development occurs in discontinuous stages—in a series of steps. These steps have been seen, however, as occurring at particular ages, with maturation occurring along one single track.

Although stratified systems theory supports this concept of discontinuity in cognitive development, it departs from current views in two respects. First, it does not associate the stages of cognitive development with particular ages. Instead, it associates these stages with maturation to particular levels of cognitive power, regardless of the age at which an individual reaches a particular level. Second, development theory tends to regard individuals as maturing in cognitive function along the same path or band, with some individuals progressing faster and further along that band than others. According to stratified systems theory, however, each individual matures in level of cognitive function not along the same band but along one of a number of maturation bands. Each maturation band is associated with a different cognitive mode, a different growth rate, and a different achievable level of cognitive power. We are dealing, therefore, with a multiple-track rather than a single-track system. These multiple tracks range from maturation bands characterized by rather slow rates of growth toward low levels of cognitive power to maturation bands characterized by much more rapid rates of development toward very much higher levels of cognitive power.

Most research on cognitive capability focuses on children and young adults. In contrast, research concerned with measuring the level of work achievable by individuals with given levels of cognitive ability can first focus on adults of all ages and then extrapolate back to children.

Level of work is measured in terms of time: the maximum targeted completion time of the objectives or goals that a person is committed to achieve. The longer the targeted completion time, the higher the person's level of capability. This measure of level of work is called the *time span of discretion* of the work; and the measure of the level of capability of individuals in terms of the maximum time spans they can achieve is called the *time frame* of the individual.

Using time-span measurement, a systematic hierarchy of levels of organization emerges at particular time spans in large-scale bureaucratic systems. There are clear-cut steps at three-month, one-year, two-year, five-year, 10-year, and 20-year time spans. These precise discontinuities can be explained in terms of discontinuities in the nature of cognitive functioning. Each successively higher level of organization is the expression of a higher and qualitatively different level of abstraction, which characterizes the particular quality of cognitive functioning that makes work possible at each higher level (Harvey and others, 1961; Streuffert and Streuffert, 1978).

The maturation bands of cognitive capability are reflected in the growth of cognitive power as measured in individual time frames. Each person's time frame, and hence cognitive power, continues to mature in a regular fashion from childhood throughout life. Individuals moving along the higher, faster tracking bands may mature to time frames of 10 and 20 years and above; individuals moving along the lower, slower tracking bands may mature to time frames of days to months. Discontinuous stages in cognitive development occur as individuals mature across the one-day, three-month, one-year, two-year, five-year, 10-year, and 20-year time-frame boundaries in adulthood.

A hierarchy of four fundamental cognitive states also underlies the discontinuities in cognitive development. These cognitive states recur in groups of four, but as increasingly complex levels of function. As individuals mature in cognitive power, they progress through each cognitive state in the first group of four. If they continue to increase in cognitive power, they will then move through each state in the second group of four but will operate at a higher level in a more complex world. The number of cognitive states and groups they move through depends on the level of cognitive power they will eventually be able to achieve in full adult maturity.

Maturation in cognitive power, as measured in time frame, is strongly constitutionally based. That is, given reasonable opportunity for encountering everyday social problems, a person's cognitive power, as measured in time frame, will mature at a predictable rate, regardless of the particular content of social, educational, or occupational opportunities. The development, however, of a person's psychological tools and orientation depends, to varying degrees, on cultural background and social opportunities. Therefore, a person's effective level of work and achievement—which combines cognitive power and psychological tools and orientation—depends on particular social and cultural circumstances.

The social and political implications of these conclusions are considerable. If it is possible to assess cognitive *power*, then it is also possible to assess the level of work individuals would be capable of carrying if they had the necessary psychological tools and orientation for particular situations. Social deprivation may inhibit the acquisition of the necessary tools and orientation and hence inhibit achievement; but, fortunately, it does not hold back the maturation of cognitive power. Steps have to be taken, therefore, to provide remedial opportunities for individuals to develop the psychological tools and orientation that can allow them to apply their cognitive powerfully and that will ultimately lead to equal opportunity regardless of race, color, sex, religion, or ethnic or social background.

Some Definitions

A key concept, and the foundation of my argument, is the concept of work itself, because I consider the development of cognitive power in relation to work. I define work as the exercise of judgment within prescribed limits (real rules and regulations) in order to achieve a goal (objective). In short, work encompasses all goal-directed behavior, in contrast to musing, reverie, fantasy, and dreaming, which are not goal directed. Thus, we may speak not only of employment work, but of recreational work, housework, artistic work, learning work—indeed, all purposive behavior.

Because work is goal directed, it exists in time. Any goal, if it is to exist in reality, must have a maximum time by which it is to be attained—its maximum targeted completion time. Without a targeted completion time, whether explicit or implicit, a goal is not a goal; it is a vague wish or desire that may be realized at some time or other but towards which no work can be organized unless a target is set.

Capability is that complex of competencies that enables an individual to work and achieve goals. It comprises a person's cognitive power and psychological tools and orientation. Cognitive power is the mental force a person can exercise in processing and organizing information and in creating a complex world; it is measurable in what I call time frame. Psychological tools and orientation include knowledge, experience, skill, emotional makeup, character, values, and approach to constructing the world.

Effective level of work is the maximum level of work individuals are able to carry in a particular function under particular circumstances, depending on their cognitive power and psychological tools and orientation. It is situation specific. Of these various components of a person's capability, only one interests us here—namely, cognitive power and its development and growth. It is my purpose in this chapter to unfold a rigorous boundary definition for cognitive functioning and an operational definition for the measurement of cognitive power in terms of time frame.

Cognitive functions exist in the general domain of our construction and patterning of the world in which we live. By amount of cognitive power, I refer to the the size or scale of the world that we are able to construct and pattern, and in which we successfully live and work. The domain is that which is sometimes described under the headings of intellectual activity and intellectual ability (but not intellectual in terms of academic, theoretical, or artistic pursuits—the currency of the "intellectual"). These functions do not refer to whatever might be rated by IQ; that rating is relevant to school performance and the learning of articulated knowledge but is only distantly relevant to the performance of work. Whatever it might be that IQ rates, it matures only to the age of 18 or so, whereas cognitive power matures in quality and grows in quantity throughout a person's life.

One last definition—*discontinuity and multi-attribute theory.* The natural sciences take for granted that qualitative changes of state, quantum changes, occur at predictable points with changes in quanity; H_2O will change in state from ice to water to vapor at critical temperatures. This assumes discontinuity between very different states. Again, this is the assumption in developmental psychology since Piaget, who saw each change in state occurring in conjunction with changes in age. I contend, however, that not only are there different states of cognitive function (that it is a multi- rather than a single-attribute phenomenon) but that the change to each different state occurs as the individual reaches a specific and predictable amount of cognitive power rather than a particular age.

Time Span and the Measurement of Level of Work

Because all work is associated with maximum target completion times for achieving particular goals, it is possible to objectively measure the longest targeted time span at which an individual is working. I call this measurement the time span of discretion at which the person is working.

What, then, is time-span measurement? Simply ask Manager A for examples of Subordinates B's assignments with long target completion times. It is the longest of these assignments that gives the time span for the role (Jaques, 1964, 1976, 1982b). Note that I am referring to targeted, rather than actual, completion times. The targets can be changed during the course of assignments; when they are, the time span may be changed as well.

The significance of time-span measurement is that it appears to relate uniquely to the felt level of work or responsibility at which a person is expected to work: the longer the time span, the greater the weight of responsibility. And the longer the time span a person can achieve, the higher the person's *level* of capability.

One source of evidence for the close relationship between time span and level of work is the extraordinarily strong correlation between time span and felt fair pay. People who are working at the same time span, regardless of occupation and pay, name the same pay levels when asked, "What do you think would be a fair total compensation for the work you are being given to do?" The correlations between measured time span in a role and a person's felt fair pay range from .86 to .92 (Richardson, 1971; Krimpas and others, 1975).

Stratification of Organization in Hierarchical Employment Systems

Studies in over 15 countries have consistently found that individuals in a role below the three-month time span feel that the occupant of the first role above the three-month time span is their real manager; between the three-month and one-year time span, the occupant of the first role above the one-year time span is felt to be the real manager;

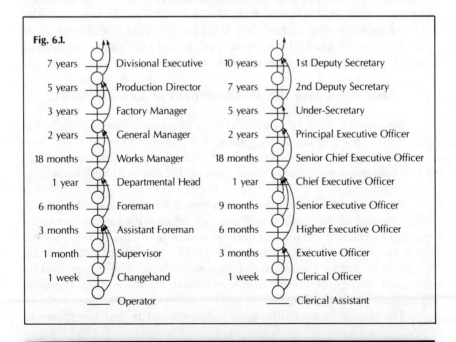

Fig. 6.1.

7 years	Divisional Executive
5 years	Production Director
3 years	Factory Manager
2 years	General Manager
18 months	Works Manager
1 year	Departmental Head
6 months	Foreman
3 months	Assistant Foreman
1 month	Supervisor
1 week	Changehand
	Operator

10 years	1st Deputy Secretary
7 years	2nd Deputy Secretary
5 years	Under-Secretary
2 years	Principal Executive Officer
18 months	Senior Chief Executive Officer
1 year	Chief Executive Officer
9 months	Senior Executive Officer
6 months	Higher Executive Officer
3 months	Executive Officer
1 week	Clerical Officer
	Clerical Assistant

between the two- and five-year time span, the occupant of the first role above the five-year time span is felt to be the real manager; between the five- and 10-year time span, the occupant of the first role above the 10-year time span is felt to be the real manager (Fig. 6.1).

This regularity has appeared consistently so far in over 100 practical field studies. It points to the existence of a structure that underlies bureaucratic organization, a substructure or a structure in depth, composed of managerial strata with consistent boundaries measured in time span, as illustrated, and inherently recognizable by employees within these strata (Fig. 6.2) (McNeil and others, 1969; Evans, 1979; Rowbottom and Billis, 1978; Jaques and others, 1978).

Fig. 6.2

Time-Span		Stratum	Industry	Army
50 yrs				
		Str-VII	Corporation	4-Star
20 yrs				
		Str-VI	Group	3-Star
10 yrs				
		Str-V	Subsidiary	2-Star
5 yrs				
		Str-IV	General Mgt	Brigade
2 yrs				
		Str-III	Unit	Battalion
1 yr				
		Str-II	Section	Company
3 mths				
		Str-I	Shop Floor	Troops

The gravamen of these findings is that there are precisely definable critical points, specified in terms of time span, at which discontinuities or quantum changes in the state of work organization occur. These discontinuities can take us directly to the identification of discontinuities in cognitive state and to a further understanding of the nature of cognitive functioning and its development.

Time Frame and Cognitive Power

Why is it that time span increases as we move to greater felt weight of responsibility and to higher and higher levels in executive systems? And why should there be a regular series of steps in organization level at particular time-span levels? The only hypothesis I have been able to construct that seems to make some sense of the findings is that the maximum time span at which a person is capable of working—that person's maximum *achieved* time span—measures and defines the person's level of cognitive power. It is this measure that I am calling the person's *time frame.*

Moreover, if there are discontinuous strata in work organizations, then there should be very different cognitive states associated with each of the bands of time frame that fall within the different organizational strata and with particular qualities in the kinds of work found in each stratum; that is, the strata with time-span bands running from one day to three months, three months to one year, and so on. The following patterns of cognitive function explain the underlying structure of organizational levels.

Stratum I. Concrete Shaping: Time Frame One Day to Three Months.

Work within this stratum takes place in relation to goals set in concretely specified terms. Tasks are carried out one at a time; the work is characterized by direct shaping of material things. As Stamp (1981) puts it, the person is anchored within concrete rules that are seen as inflexible.

This is the kind of work carried out by manual shop workers and office clerical staff. They operate by losing themselves in the activity. Improvement occurs with accumulated practice and experience. These experiences may be articulated as new ways of going about things, but they cannot themselves be detached and related to one another away from the concrete work setting. Development and improvement require the direct interaction between thought and immediate, concrete, ongoing experience.

This stratum also encompasses the work of supervisory assistants to first-line managers. Such assistants can watch over the work being done by Stratum I personnel, point out what needs to be done, and help and train by pointing to errors and by demonstrating the correct methods.

Stratum II. Task Definition: Time Frame Three Months to One Year.

Work within this stratum starts out with the ability to reflect on our own work as we carry it out and the ability to articulate what is going on. In addition, we can collect these articulated experiences so as to accumulate knowledge about aggregates of tasks. It thus becomes possible to work with these ideas in themselves, away from the actual work situation, and to develop and formulate new ideas and methods for overcoming problems and improving one's work.

Individuals who work in Stratum II are able to deal with goal ambiguity; as they deal with an ambiguous goal, they can work on clarifying it further by detached reflection while working toward it. Stamp (1981) describes the phenomenon of a person using judgment and action within rules in such a way as to be able to handle ambiguity by separating situations and articulating their differences. This facility for reflective articulation enables the first-line manager at this stratum to delegate to subordinates new ways of solving problems.

The scale of organization is that of the mutual knowledge group. The circumstances must allow the manager to sustain direct contact with his or her immediate subordinates in order to accumulate the necessary experience with their problems to be able to exercise his or her ability in reflective articulation.

Or, to take an example of a nonmanager: a social worker doing a family case workup will have certain things in mind in talking with members of the family but at the same time will reflectively determine what further kinds of information and interpretation are needed. This work would be very different, for example, from that carried out by a social work aide operating at Stratum I who visits a family with a specified set of questions.

Stratum III. Task Extrapolation: Time Frame One Year to Two Years.

Here the situation involves an individual faced by two things at the same time: first, by a known workload stretching from, say, three to six months; and, second, by an as yet unknown but probable workload lasting up to an additional year. The person must therefore make trade-offs in planning and in work between the requirements of carrying out the known workload and preparing for changes in the nature of the workload, which must be predicted trends. Stamp (1981) describes this stratum as work that calls for the ability to extrapolate from given rules.

This stratum is that of the departmental or unit manager, with a staff of 200 to 300 people. The scale is that of the mutual recognition group; that is, everyone in the unit can recognize everyone else as working in the same place. It is the largest scale of institution without anonymity. In military terms, it is the level of the Army battalion of 600 or the Navy destroyer of 400, the larger numbers being possible because mutual recognition can be sustained through the 168-hours-a-week working and living contact among the members of the unit.

For individual specialists in nonmanagerial positions at this level, such as scientists or independent professionals, the cognitive mode of operation is the same as for unit managers. Independent professionals—lawyers, say, or physiotherapists—at this level are not only able to handle a case load extending over some months (as for the Stratum II case-worker) but are also capable of developing their practices by extending their network of clients for a year or more beyond their present load.

Scientists at this level, for instance, are able to carry out research tasks specified for them for periods of some months, as would be required for Stratum II scientists. But they are able to do more. They can follow the trends in the research literature and work out a sequence of studies for a year or more that follow from those trends. They can envisage new studies by extrapolation from the trend.

Because the individual's work extends from a solid known workbase to an emerging load, the probable load can be planned for and coped with by linear (or serial) extrapolation. The capability to work by *linear extrapolation* is the *sine qua non* of the cognitive state of individuals who are able to work in the one- to two-year zone.

Stratum IV. Transform Systems: Time Frame Two Years to Five Years.

The complexity of cognitive work jumps one full step from the fine-tuning of a given linear extrapolative system to the consideration of alternative Stratum III systems that might get the work done better. This level requires the ability to compare known systems with one another, usually in pairs. It does not call for the development of as yet unknown systems. As Stamp (1981) describes it, there is the maintenance of a pattern rule structure within which hypotheses are explicitly stated and tested.

Take, for instance, the general manager of a foundry, rough-machining shop, and finished-machining shop. He needs to continually review whether to sustain his existing operations by replacing worn-out tools and equipment or whether to restructure any or all of his shops into a different kind of producing entity. His review will be based on his comparisons of his shops with other existing systems.

As another example, research professors will unfold alternative sets of hypotheses, conclusions, or consequences from a given theoretical context within which they work. But they will not disturb the theory, and indeed will strive to conserve it, for they may become anxious at the prospect of losing the support of a theory they understand.

Similarly, Army brigade commanders need to be capable of modifying battalion task forces in action to meet a new or unexpected situation. They will expect their task force commanders to operate their battalions as effectively as possible in their original form and in their new form as well.

Competence in the development of alternative systems by means of paired comparison of known systems, then, is the substance of the quality of cognitive functioning at Stratum IV in the two- to five-year time frame.

Stratum V. Shaping Whole Systems: Time Frame Five to Ten Years.

At the fifth level a key boundary zone is reached. This zone is at the upper limit of human capability to function by forecasting what the future might hold and how it should be planned for. Above this stratum there must be a transformation to constructing the future rather than forecasting it.

At Stratum V there is a return to the hands-on shaping that characterizes Stratum I, but the entities being shaped are now complex social institutions or general theories rather than material things. The individual cannot only operate a complex system but can modify the boundaries of that system and cope with the second- and third-order consequences that inevitably arise. In Stamp's (1981) terms, things are explicitly seen as interdependent; to change one part is to change the whole. Individuals begin to define situations for themselves and make the necessary rules.

An example would be the chief executive officer of a subsidiary of a large corporation whose role is to shape and reshape from within the business he or she controls. He or she may push out its boundaries in one place into new market opportunities or product development. But he or she will have to make the necessary consequential adjustments by, say, pulling in its market boundaries elsewhere or modifying certain production resources.

The same shaping-from-within approach will inform scientific research in this zone of cognitive competence. The individual deals with theories not as though they were sacrosanct but as contexts to be used for giving shape to the development of studies. These contexts may themselves be reshaped and modified in light of experience and research.

It is striking that human activity gets organized in such a manner that the largest of projects—such as the building of dams, battleships, or power stations—fall within the five- to 10-year limits (usually six to seven years). If specific projects with budgetable outcomes are established with targeted completion times beyond 10 years, they turn out to be difficult to control. Instead, they tend to be broken down and planned in phases of less than 10 years as, for example, in the building of cathedrals. Thus, the construction of nuclear power stations has become extremely difficult to control; although it is physically possible to build them in five to seven years, it is no longer possible to do so in under 12 to 15 years because of the complexity of regulatory requirements.

Stratum VI. Defining Whole Systems in the Wide World: Time Frame 10 to 20 Years.

The move in work across the 10-year boundary is accompanied by a dramatic change. Instead of working within complex institutions or general theories, which themselves exist in a whole-world environment, the individual now oversees and changes institutions or theories from the outside. This world is no longer one in which the "future" is merely to be forecast by predicting likely trends in events and behavior of other people. It is becoming a world that might be fashioned and modified, despite what is going on, because the necessary resources and individual capabilities have entered into the situation.

The work requirement is again that of the reflective articulation that characterized Stratum II. But the situation now requires the operation of institutions and the fibrillating infinity of restlessly changing variables within which they exist and function. These variables are political, economic, social, technological, and intellectual (PESTI).

Living and working in the worldwide environment calls for an ability to impose upon one's world a cognitive ordering within which what is deemed most relevant can be sorted out from the rest, priorities kept in a continual state of good repair, and as friendly an environment as possible sustained. Competence in networking with key individuals in many fields in one's own and other countries is an essential quality of capability at this level.

For example, a strategic business unit executive vice president of a large corporation oversees 14 subsidiary trading business units, each directed by a vice president. Each business unit is a Stratum V whole-system unified command. The role of the executive vice president is to network within the PESTI world, to screen vice presidents from the continual shifting of the PESTI world, and to hold off the irrelevant while admitting the important. The executive vice president will determine which matters the vice presidents should be concerned with and which they should disregard for the time being. Those matters might include a technical breakthrough at a foreign university, a political coup in Africa, a new adolescent fad in Australia, border incidents in the Far East, elections in Japan, a hold up in economic growth in the United States, or rumors of a competitor's new product. The executive vice president, then, will help sustain a living context for his or her vice presidents and take an active part in the modification and development of corporate strategy.

To operate at this level of reflective articulation calls for what is often referred to as a "conceptual approach." This means that, in the over-10-year term, all the pieces necessary for the completion of a project or an acquisition will not be immediately available. It is possible to get or negotiate the missing pieces (via basic analysis, research and development, or investigation), but there is still work to be done to put the pieces together to reach a solution. The combinatorial conception has yet to be found and articulated—as in, for example, carrying responsibility for getting and putting into operation a new fleet of aircraft for 1997, when negotiations with government authorities over regulations have not yet been completed and are holding up detailed specifications.

Stratum VII. Extrapolative Development of Whole Systems: Time Frame 20 Years Plus.

Here we move into the full corporate area. It is the level concerned with either (1) managing a system that can carry out the development, formation, and construction of complex Stratum V institutions; (2) the transformation of existing institutions; or (3) the divestment of such institutions. The scientific equivalent would be the construction of theories as a specific objective in its own right.

Stratum VII, therefore, is the work of constructing institutions and theories and placing them into society at large. The mode is extrapolative, as in Stratum III, but it is highly discretionary extrapolation in that it is concerned with constructing the future rather than forecasting it. The individual works with a number of existing institutions or theories, but the art is to understand which new ones might be needed to develop and oversee the extension from the present so as to fill the gaps, and to provide society with new concepts, new research and development programs, and new ideas. Thus, an overarching vision is set out that provides a 20- to 25-year working orientation within which subordinates or next-level-down scientific colleagues can work.

One might expect these very long time frames to produce great feelings of uncertainty in the people who work at those levels. But the opposite is the case. People at Stratum VII and above are literally engaged in constructing the future within which we will live. They are putting in train now those things and ideas that will become part of the world 20 years forward and beyond. Far from feeling uncertain about that world, they feel a sense of familiarity with what they are creating.

A Quintave Theory of Cognitive Development

There are two phenomena embedded in the foregoing descriptions. The first is a hierarchy of four cognitive states: shaping, reflective articulation, linear extrapolation, and alternative systems. Each state characterizes the work of a particular work stratum; for example, Stratum IV: alternative systems, two- to five-year time span. The second phenomenon is that each of these four different cognitive states may reappear in a higher stratum in a more complex or higher-level setting. These two features are illustrated in Figure 6.3.

Figure 6.3.

Stratum	Time	Description
	50Y	
Stratum VII		*Extrapolative* Development of Whole Systems
	20Y	
Stratum VI		*Defining* Whole Systems in World Environment
	10Y	
Stratum V		*Shaping* Whole Systems from Within
	5Y	
Stratum IV		*Transforming* Concrete Systems
	2Y	
Stratum III		*Extrapolation* in Concrete Systems
	1Y	
Stratum II		*Defining* Tasks
	3M	
Stratum I		*Shaping* Concrete Things
	1D	

This scheme can be further extended from data obtained by work on the assessment of mental handicap carried out by Macdonald and Couchman (Macdonald, 1978). They found that mentally handicapped individuals manifest cognitive approaches to work that are strikingly similar to the cognitive modes described above but manifest them in relation to a much more limited and concrete world and requiring the continual assistance of an aide. Thus, in their schema, the Level 1 cognitive state is one in which the individual sits and rocks and does nothing unless prompted by an aide to set goals and decide how to achieve them. For example, if the individual is hungry, he cannot be sure what to do about it. But if an aide should suggest a sandwich and show him how to get it, he is, with help, able to feed himself. Given both a goal and a path, he is able to *shape* an action.

At Level 2 the individual is able to *reflect* and to form and *define* a path if he is aided to construct a goal. Thus, if the aide suggests a sandwich, the individual can reach for it without having to be shown how to do it.

At Level 3 the individual is able to choose both a goal and a path to it; but once committed to the goal and path, he is involved in a rigid and inflexible *linear action* (extrapolation) from which he cannot be shifted, slowed or stopped. He cannot entertain alternatives. This level is that of the same handicapped individuals who are prone to temper outbursts if attempts are made to dissuade them from doing what they have determined to do.

At Level 4 a more flexible pattern of behavior emerges. The possibility exists that there might be *alternatives* to a desired or chosen course of action. As a result, the individual who can function at this level is more flexible, malleable, and socializable. He understands that other people may have alternate points of view or desires and that one can *transform* one's own views.

At Level 5 we find individuals able to function at the *concrete shaping* level as unskilled or semiskilled operators or clerks. They are capable of living on their own. If they are considered mentally handicapped it is because they were put in that stream in early childhood and have been rendered dependent by institutional care. They can, without much difficulty, be aided to assume an independent role in life.

We have, then, an apparent recurrence of our four modes of cognitive functioning: shaping, defining, extrapolating, and transforming. But they occur in a more restricted form in which individuals must depend on aides in order to be able to function at all. The world in which they operate is made up of very concrete items completely bounded within the physically present situation.

If we put these findings and hypotheses together, we get the following pattern. The fifth level of mental handicap overlaps and coincides with the first level of cognitive function (Stratum I) in ordinary work systems. When we move up to Stratum V we find that it is both the top of the five strata making up the organization levels of whole systems and at the same time the bottom or the beginning of a yet higher series of shaping, reflective articulation, and linear programming of the corporate or general theory construction levels of organization.

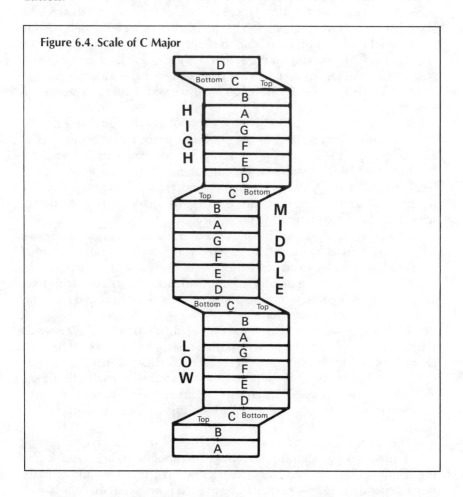

Figure 6.4. Scale of C Major

This pattern is very much like the octave of the western musical scale. An octave is, in fact, a seven-note scale and not an eight-note scale; for example, in the scale of C major, the first note, C, reappears as the eighth, which is then the first note of the next higher octave. The note C is always both the first note and the eighth in the scale.

Using this analog, we derive a quintave pattern of cognitive states, with the four states recurring in groups of five but operating in increasingly complex worlds. The first cognitive state—that of shaping—acts as the dual bottom and top of each quintave, as shown in Figure 6.5.

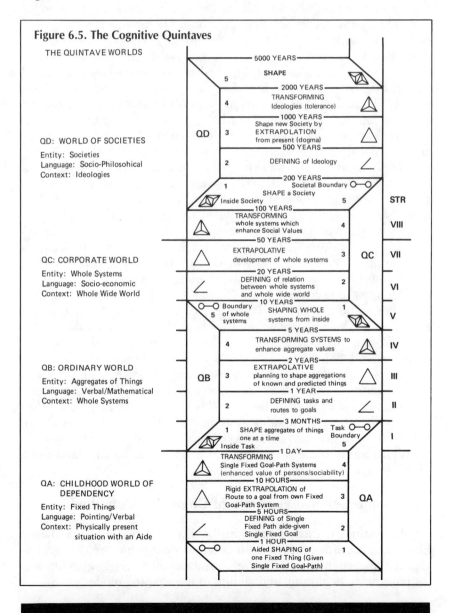

Figure 6.5. The Cognitive Quintaves

THE QUINTAVE WORLDS

QD: WORLD OF SOCIETIES

Entity: Societies
Language: Socio-Philosohical
Context: Ideologies

QC: CORPORATE WORLD

Entity: Whole Systems
Language: Socio-economic
Context: Whole Wide World

QB: ORDINARY WORLD

Entity: Aggregates of Things
Language: Verbal/Mathematical
Context: Whole Systems

QA: CHILDHOOD WORLD OF DEPENDENCY

Entity: Fixed Things
Language: Pointing/Verbal
Context: Physically present situation with an Aide

QD

5 — 5000 YEARS — SHAPE
4 — 2000 YEARS — TRANSFORMING Ideologies (tolerance)
3 — 1000 YEARS — Shape new Society by EXTRAPOLATION from present (dogma)
2 — 500 YEARS — DEFINING of Ideology
1 — 200 YEARS — Societal Boundary — SHAPE a Society — Inside Society — 5 — STR

QC

4 — 100 YEARS — TRANSFORMING whole systems which enhance Social Values — VIII
3 — 50 YEARS — EXTRAPOLATIVE development of whole systems — VII
2 — 20 YEARS — DEFINING of relation between whole systems and whole wide world — VI
1 — 10 YEARS — SHAPING WHOLE systems from inside — Boundary of whole systems — 5 — V

QB

4 — 5 YEARS — TRANSFORMING SYSTEMS to enhance aggregate values — IV
3 — 2 YEARS — EXTRAPOLATIVE planning to shape aggregations of known and predicted things — III
2 — 1 YEAR — DEFINING tasks and routes to goals — II
1 — 3 MONTHS — SHAPE aggregates of things one at a time — Task Boundary — 5 — Inside Task — I

QA

4 — 1 DAY — TRANSFORMING Single Fixed Goal-Path Systems (enhanced value of persons/sociability)
3 — 10 HOURS — Rigid EXTRAPOLATION of Route to a goal from own Fixed Goal-Path System
2 — 5 HOURS — DEFINING of Single Fixed Path aide-given Single Fixed Goal
1 — 1 HOUR — Aided SHAPING of one Fixed Thing (Given Single Fixed Goal-Path)

But what then might occur below QA-1 and above QC-3? I would think there would be no possibility of an individual remaining alive at levels below QA-1. The newborn would hardly survive through infancy.

At the other end of the scale, however, above QC-3, there is plenty of room for growth. QC-4 would be the level of cognitive function for Stratum VIII in a corporate organization. There are a few super-corporations that in fact do have a Stratum VIII. They are the corporations that have been built up and led by recognized outstanding individuals, such as Vail of AT&T, Sloan of General Motors, and Matsushita of Matsushita Electric. An interesting thing about such individuals is that they are not only capable of developing alternative systems for the establishment of large corporations but are almost uniformly concerned about and interested in the relation between their corporations and the society in which they live.

This concern about societies gives a possible clue to the nature of Quintave D. Referring back to QB-4 (transforming systems of production), we see that it looks upward toward the Stratum V work of QB-5 in that it is concerned with volume of output and its cost and is therefore involved in notional profitability, which becomes actual profitability at Stratum V. By the same token, if Stratum VIII (QC-4) is looking up to Stratum IX (QC-5/QD-1) in its social orientation, then QD-1 might be concerned with the shaping of societies.

This last conclusion, in fact, leads to speculation on a possible hypothesis about Quintave D. We encounter at these levels the rare individuals who actually create societies. The QD-1 individual is capable of shaping societies. QD-2 is capable not only of shaping a society but of defining how a society is shaped and what kind of society she is trying to shape. QD-3 is a linear societal-system creator but sees no alternatives; she is the creator of dogma—far-reaching in social impact but dogma nonetheless. QD-4 is able to value and teach toleration and to transform value systems and dogma as well as set up alternatives to her own creation. I leave it to the reader to try to fit individuals into these categories and to speculate on the nature of a possible Quintave E.

Some General Features of Cognitive Complexity

In summary, then, I have outlined a stratified systems theory about four cognitive modes of functioning and the hierarchical grouping of those cognitive modes into an ascending series of quintaves, each quintave beginning and ending in the shaping mode.

There are, thus, two stepwise movements in the extension of cognitive complexity. First, each step in cognitive state represents a qualitative step in extension of cognitive complexity, in that there is a jump in both the number and the range of entities that can be handled by being encompassed within the context of successively more extensive categories—that is, in the move from entity to aggregates of entities, to linear series of probable entities, to alternative systems of entities.

Second, there is a stepwise movement in quintaves of entities, each quintave representing the movement into successively more complex and more extended worlds—that is, from Quintave A, the dependent world of children, of closed categories of concrete things; to Quintave B, the ordinary world of open categories of things and people; to Quintave C, the world where people and things exist as patterns of complex systems and general theories; to Quintave D, the world that is constructed in the form of whole societies with everything else as subsets within societies.

The shaping mode occurs as a duality: it operates in part in the world of the quintave of which it is the top mode. At the same time it picks up the quality of the world of the quintave of which it is the bottom mode. This duality helps to explain a number of commonly occurring phenomena, as illustrated in the following examples.

People at the lower levels of mode QA-5/QB-1 (shaping at the top of Quintave A and bottom of Quintave B) tend to be rated either as high-grade mentally handicapped or as unskilled workers. The difference depends on whether they grew up and were socialized in special schools and homes for the mentally handicapped, which reinforced their dependence on others and the QA-5 outlook, or whether they grew up in their own homes with other children of their own or higher levels of capability and had opportunities for developing their maximum independence in the QB-1 mode. By the same token, individuals who function at levels of abstraction at the lower half of the QA-5/QB-1 mode may require an organization at work in which their first-line manager is assisted by supervisory assistants who can be continuously present at the workplace to keep an eye on things and give immediate help when necessary.

Another example is one cited earlier—that of vice presidents of Stratum V subsidiary business units in large corporations who operate in the dual mode QB-5/QC-1. The common experience is that of recurring reorganizations that shift from so-called centralization, in which the vice president is constrained within narrow policies from above that prohibit effective work, to decentralization, in which the vice president is suddenly given such great freedom as to be able to act against the interests of the corporation. The solution to this damaging oscillation is to recognize the duality of the QB-5/QC-1 cognitive state: the vice president is accountable for shaping a unified system while accounting for upward inputs into the corporate strategic policy within which he or she must work. When the dual nature of the Stratum V QB-5/QC-1 role is understood, the concepts of centralization and decentralization can be recognized as a false dichotomy, and the need for such a dichotomy disappears.

Another example is what may occur at QC-4 and the movement toward QC-5/QD-1. The QC-4 mode operates at Stratum VIII, which is the very top of the very largest corporations. The chairpersons and chief executive officers at this level are generally well known in their own countries and are often known throughout the world. They build up the large corporations and then stop, although it would be my hypothesis that collegial groups of such individuals could, if they so wished, construct massively larger corporations. What they do instead, however, is express their potential capability in the development of relationships between their corporations and the society around them. They have a profound impact on their societies, for better or for worse. On the one hand, they may strive to develop international cartels, with impact on international political relationships. Or at the other extreme, they may, like Matsushita, strive to orient their corporations toward "the peace, health, and prosperity" of their own nation and the world. Either option is a foretaste of the Quintave D orientation of which such individuals are inevitably potentially capable—an orientation that drives them toward an interest in shaping societies themselves and pulls them away from what they feel as the boredom of the mere construction of ever-larger institutions within societies. It is likely that Stratum IX enterprises do not emerge at QC-5/QD-1 because this interest in the shaping of society itself becomes dominant.

Maturation of Cognitive Power: The Growth of Time Frame in Individuals

Cognitive power is but one component of the attributes that form a person's ability to work. The other attributes include *knowledge, experience, skill, temperament, character, values,* and *type or quality of articulation.* We are concerned here only with cognitive functioning. It is not that cognitive equipment (knowledge, experience, and skill) is not important, but how such equipment is acquired is very different from the regular patterns of maturation of cognitive functioning. The question of how temperament and values change with time will also be left aside. Let us turn, then, to the development of cognitive functioning in its own right.

It is unlikely that human beings are born fully matured in cognitive power. How then does the process of maturation occur? The theory of discontinuity of cognitive state and of quintaves suggests a number of different questions that need to be teased out from one another.

One question is whether people who eventually mature to be able to operate in mode QC-2 at Stratum VI, for example, show signs of not yet matured QC-2 potential earlier in life. If they do, when do signs of QC-2 potential first show? Sometime in childhood? In early adulthood? Throughout life? At different times in different individuals? At the same time in all potential QC-2 individuals?

Another question is whether an individual's potential to function at a particular cognitive level or in a particular cognitive mode is inborn—constitutionally given—or whether the potential *per se* can be modified by education or occupational or social opportunity. If it can be modified, by how much? Is everyone capable of developing to any cognitive level? Or is there a constitutional base that sets the maximum limit of growth and development? These questions are, of course, among the politically loaded issues of developmental theory and need to be addressed with great care. In order to proceed systematically, let me develop further the concept of the time frame of the individual.

At any particular point in people's careers there is a maximum time span at which any given person can work. If people are employed at levels of work below that maximum time span, they feel their capabilities are being underutilized and experience boredom and frustration. If people are employed at levels of work above that maximum time span, they become disorganized, anxious, and are unable to cope. If people are fortunate enough to be employed at levels of work that coincide with the maximum time spans they are capable of achieving, then they feel comfortably employed. As long as their work is of interest and they have the appropriate knowledge, skill, and temperament, they will derive satisfaction from that work (Jaques, 1976, 1968; Evans, 1979; and Homa, 1967).

It is this maximum time span at which a person is able to work at a given point in time that I refer to as time frame. This time frame gives a measure of the extent of a person's temporal horizon at that time (Jaques, 1982b). The temporal horizon sets the limits of the world

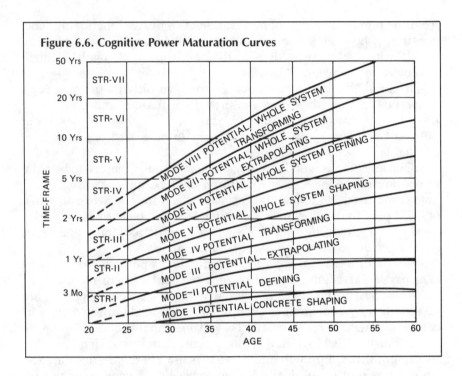

Figure 6.6. Cognitive Power Maturation Curves

of purpose and intention within which people live and construct patterns and organize their active lives and aspirations.

The curves in Figure 6.6 set out my hypothesis about the rate of maturation of time frame. The curves express the rates of maturation and growth of the cognitive power of individuals. This hypothesis was originally derived from a regularity noted in the real earning progressions of individuals (that is, their earnings corrected to a common base for movements in the earnings index) in over a dozen different countries (Jaques, 1961, 1964; Evans, 1979).

My hypothesis was that the regularity in the trend of the earnings progressions reflected a regular trend in the growht of level of cognitive function in the individuals in the samples. Or, as I would now express it, the growth in earnings reflected a drive in the individuals toward achieving a growth in level of work, which was in turn the expression of their growth in time frame.

That there is, in fact, a growth in time frame that corresponds to these curves has been demonstrated in a number of studies. In one study, I tracked the careers of almost 200 individuals for periods of between 18 and 25 years. At various times during those periods, I was able to obtain measures of time spans at which individuals were work-ing, their actual pay and their felt fair pay, and their sense of the degree of fit between their level of capability and their level of work. When there was a felt mismatch, we were able to get measures of the level of work in positions that the individuals felt would be just right for them.

Tom Kohler of UCLA, who analyzed these data, found a strong regularity in the "comfort curves," as he has called them, of individ-uals. These comfort curves conform very tightly to the progression curves of my hypothesis, some 95 percent of the actual curves staying within the bands designated Mode I, II, and so forth on my chart. The general trend of these comfort curves is shown in Figure 6.7. (Kohler is now preparing the results of his study for publication.)

Let us examine these curves more closely, starting with the sig-nificance of the modal bands. The horizontal lines running across the figures at the time spans of one day, three months, one year, two years, five years, 10 years, and 20 years, set out the boundaries of Stratum I through VII. The bands have been picked out in such a way that each one encompasses all the time-frame maturation curves, which reach the relevant stratum at full maturity. Thus, the band designated Mode III encompasses all the maturation curves that eventually reach Stra-tum III.

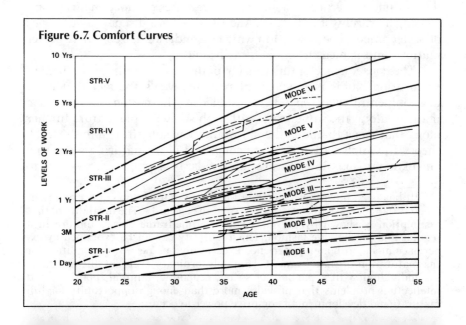

Figure 6.7. Comfort Curves

Individuals at the higher modes (V through VIII) do not reach full maturity by the maximum age of 55 years allowed for on the chart in Figure 6.7. The earnings progression data suggest that people of these very high potential levels of capability do not reach full maturity in cognitive level by normal retirement age. And, indeed, at the very highest levels it would appear that individuals are afflicted by senile deterioration and death before their potential cognitive power can reach full maturity—a hypothesis that is supported by the careers of many of the very greatest composers, artists, judges, and outstanding leaders in other fields.

These hypotheses are, of course, inconsistent with the findings from IQ ratings, which suggest full maturation by the age of 18 of whatever it is that IQ rates. The fact that IQ matures fully at such an early age emphasizes the gross limitations of IQ rating in relation to giving any indication of cognitive development.[1]

A Multiple-Track Theory of Development

It may now be apparent that we have constructed a third group of discontinuities. The first is a discontinuous hierarchy of levels in the structure of organizations. The second comprises discontinuities in the nature of cognitive capability in individuals, reflected in a discontinuous hierarchy of four cognitive states grouped in an encompassing hierarchy of quintaves. And the third is a discontinuous series of developmental bands within which the individual's cognitive power matures and is measurable by time frame.

The consequence of this third hypothesis about discontinuities in maturation bands is of some interest. It reveals the fact that most developmental theory has been wedded to the notion that everyone matures along the same track, although some people mature further along that track than do others. I would now substitute a multi-track theory in which individuals are conceived of as maturing along any one of several possible maturation bands. It is as though we were to

---

[1]It has been put to me that the time-frame maturation curves represent "merely" an increase in experience beyond the age of 18. The invalidity of that assumption is shown by the fact that the time-frame curves mature in a regular and predictable fashion. This regularity cannot be explained by experience alone, although experience is certainly one necessary condition for the maturation of time frame. Fortunately, ordinary everyday life confronts the individual with a panoply of social, economic, familial, political, and intellectual problems that provides more than enough opportunity for full maturational development of cognitive power to occur.

move from a single-track railway system to a multiple-track railway system: a number of new explanatory principles become available.

There are two very general implications of this construction: (1) each person will mature in level of cognitive power as measured by time frame within one particular maturation band; and (2) in so doing, each person will cross a number of work strata, each stratum being characterized by a particular cognitive state. The greater the cognitive power of the individual, the greater the number of strata to be crossed. There are complexities here that need to be carefully teased out and examined.

For example: say on Figure 6.6 Individual A has matured to a time frame of three years at the age of 31. There are two points to note: first, she will be able to work in Stratum IV at that age, and second, she is maturing in the Mode VII cognitive band and will have the potential to reach Stratum VII by sometime between the ages of 60 and 65. It may be noted that Stratum IV implies work in cognitive state QB-4 and Stratum VII implies work in cognitive state QC-3.

We now encounter a prime question inherent in the theory of stratified systems: how do individuals of high-level potential function at lower levels while they are maturing? For example, what would be the cognitive state of A at age 31—Mode QB-4 (transforming systems) or Mode QC-3 (extrapolation)? And how would A compare in cognitive state with, say, B, who is 55 years of age and also at three years time frame and who, according to our theory, would be both operating at QB-4 and fully matured in QB-4, so that there would be no inconsistency between current cognitive state and potential cognitive state?

The answer to this question is an interesting one that has been worked out in field studies carried out over the past ten years by Gillian Stamp. Building on work done by John Isaac, Brian O'Connor, and Roland Gibson (Isaac and O'Connor, 1978; Gibson and Isaac, 1978), Stamp has developed an instrument for the assessment of level of cognitive power, both current and potential (Stamp, 1978). This instrument, which she has named Career Path Appreciation (CPA), comprises a card-sorting procedure based on the Bruner cards (Bruner and others, 1966), a choice of phrase cards describing various preferred ways of working, and a brief interview to ascertain the time span of work at which the individual currently feels comfortable.

With this hour-long procedure, Stamp has been able to ascertain both individuals' current time frame and the dynamic strategies they use in approaching problem solving. She is able to place individuals at low, middle, or high in a particular stratum and, by the some token, in a particular cognitive maturation band.

Thus, for A and B above, Stamp would be able to place A in mid-Stratum IV and Maturation band VII, and B in mid-Stratum IV and Maturation band IV. Her studies show that both A and B would be currently operating in cognitive mode QB-4, but with a difference. B's performance would consistently show a QB-4 transforming approach set firmly in Quintave B with little if any comprehension of how to go about working at any higher level: his temporal horizon would end abruptly at about three to four years. A's performance, by contrast, would be expressed in a QB-4 transforming approach, but it would contain signs of QB-5 and higher on the phrase cards. Moreover, in interview, A would manifest clear signs of comprehension of QC-VII modes of working and, most striking of all, would have already taken for granted that people might be engaged in constructing worlds 10, 20, and 25 years ahead, even though accurate forecasting could not produce such temporal horizons.

In short, Stamp concluded that individuals will express their currently matured time frame in their work but at the same time will show evidence of comprehending their potential cognitive mode and temporal horizon. I have had extensive experience with this two-dimensional phenomenon. The temporal horizons of men and women in the younger age groups, for example, are of particular interest. The high-potential group readily understands the world in long-time horizons, even though they are not yet mature enough to work at that scale of temporal extension. By contrast, the lower-potential individuals simply do not see the more extensive context.

Development of Cognitive Complexity in Childhood

How then does cognitive functioning, as defined here, develop in childhood? We are just getting studies of this question under way, within the following hypotheses.

I have replotted the time-frame-progression array set out in Figure 6.6 onto a double logarithmic scale to make it possible to do a crude extrapolation of these curves back to earliest infancy. On the assumption that the progression would be in line with the sigmoid curves characteristic of biological development, I drew the extrapolated curves as shown in Figure 6.8. Note that the higher the cognitive mode, the later in life a person's cognitive power continues to mature and increase.

It then occurred to me that the work of Macdonald and Couchman gave a lead into the nature of cognitive capability in children. Their findings about cognitive levels in a population of mentally handi-

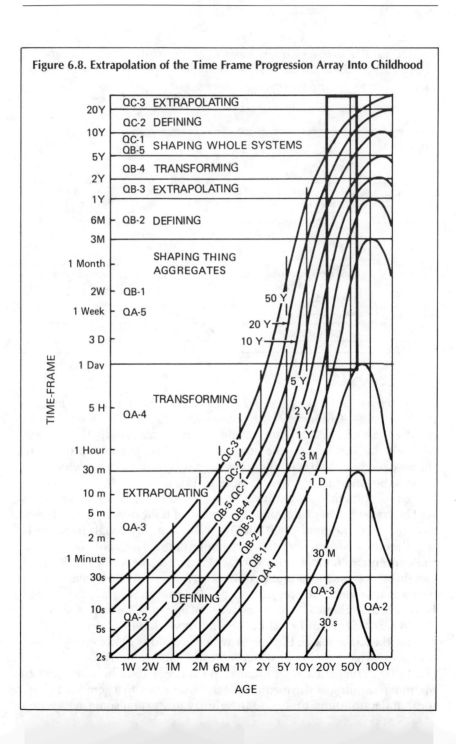

Figure 6.8. Extrapolation of the Time Frame Progression Array Into Childhood

capped adults are very suggestive of the cognitive modes found in infancy and early childhood in the type of population studied by Piaget. The following correspondences occur:

Figure 6.9		
	QUINTAVE THEORY	**PIAGET'S THEORY**
QA-5/QB-1	Ability to operate in an adult world at Stratum I	Period of formal operations; the ability to reason by hypothesis
QA-4	First stage of concern about alternatives and about the interests of others	Period of concrete operations; combination, dissociation, ordering and correspondences that acquire the form of reversible systems
QA-3	Rigid fixation on own goals; disregard of others' needs; tantrums if stopped	Period of pre-operational thought
QA-2	Primitive reflective articulation	Sensory motor period
QA-1	Complete dependence on an aide	

The hypothesis is suggested that the bottom quintave of the cognitive modes—Quintave A—expresses the stages of development in children. Some children may develop much more rapidly than others through the stages; and the stages extend throughout adulthood in the so-called mentally handicapped—that is, among those who never develop beyond the first four cognitive states.

On this further assumption that the Quintave A cognitive states will be traversed by children in the course of their development, I have hypothesized the modes within QA, as shown. My rough hypothesis was that the children with the very highest potential would cross from the egocentric, temper-tantrum QA-3 stage to the socializable QA-4 capability of understanding; that others may have alternatives, at perhaps six months to one year of age; and that that same stage might be reached at about five to seven years of age in those with the potential to reach Stratum I or II in their adult working careers.

By the same token, the age at which a child is able to understand and act on the meaning of yesterday, today, and tomorrow might turn out to be diagnostically of great importance. I refer here not just to an understanding of the meaning of the words but to a genuine behavioral understanding; that is, to the ability to start on some activity on one day with the realization that it will certainly take until the following day to complete it, and to carry the activity through without getting into a fit of rage and abandoning it when bedtime arrives with the project only half finished. My hypothesized developmental curves would predict that Mode VII children will be able to handle the tomorrow time span by the age of three; Mode IV children by the age of six; and Mode I persons by the age of 21.

We have just begun a research project in which we will be assessing five-year-old, 10-year-old, and 15-year-old children to discover the nature and maturation pattern of cognitive power at those ages. Our initial studies include boys and girls from different social and ethnic backgrounds. The hypotheses are at least precise enough to be falsified, reinforced, or modified.

A Note on "Predestination"

Hypotheses of the kind I have outlined about intellectual or cognitive capability and its development seem inevitably to give rise to criticism on political grounds. They are held to be politically reactionary on racial grounds or of being neofeudal in the sense of putting individuals into fixed slots in life. These criticisms are of substantial importance and warrant comment.

As far as racial issues are concerned, it is gratifying to be able to report that Stamp has begun to obtain evidence that her assessment procedure can be used without modification regardless of the subject's cultural, social, racial, or economic background. It would appear—as I would most certainly hypothesize—that individuals mature in time frame and thus in cognitive power under the impact of the problems presented by everyday life, regardless of whether those problems have had to be faced under the exigencies of school learning or under the exigencies of survival in a setting of social and educational deprivation. Who is to say which is likely to provide the greater stimulus?

Let me emphasize that I am talking about maturation of cognitive power only. I am not talking about the social and economic opportunity to exercise that cognitive power in education or employment and thereby develop the psychological tools and orientation needed to advance in our society. If these hypotheses about development turn out to be valid, it would mean that whether or not individuals have adequate social, educational, or occupational opportunities for developing particular psychological tools and orientation, their cognitive power will develop nonetheless. If, however, they do not have the opportunity to learn and to develop the appropriate psychological tools and orientation for work that matches their capability, people will fall behind in their ability to compete in their societies. At the very least, they will be frustrated and fed up and feel unjustly treated.

Moreover, if the discrepancies between cognitive power, on the one hand, and appropriate psychological tools, orientation, and work opportunities, on the other, are great, people will fall seriously behind in status and in achievement. Some will work zealously to overcome this disadvantage, and a few will become social reformers. But many others will become alienated and may seek antisocial or delinquent outlets for their ability, or instigate more or less violent social change. It is precisely because maturation in cognitive power occurs despite social and economic opportunity that social alienation and resentment can occur, led by those with the highest levels of underutilized cognitive power. Any society, to be a decent society, must provide the opportunity for individuals to gain the tools and orientation necessary for them to be able to use their cognitive powers to the full and must ensure the provision of full employment opportunities for all (Jaques, 1982a).

Indeed, it is the viewpoint that educational and social opportunity are necessary for the maturation of a person's level of cognitive power that I find difficult to understand. For that view contains the implicit assumption that under generations of subjugation with social, educational, and economic deprivation, subject peoples would have produced populations of intellectual morons. Human nature and the maturation of cognitive power appear, fortunately, to be more resilient than that.

Finally, I would note that the assessments of cognitive power that I have described are a very far cry from the world of IQ ratings. My whole orientation is toward the performance of individuals in planning and carrying out goal-directed activities and, thus, in constructing their own worlds. This orientation has little relation to IQ ratings, which fail to adequately separate individual cognitive power from culturally dominated cognitive equipment. Such ratings lean too heavily on culturally learned answers and language and on ability to learn what is taught in schools, whether or not the individual has been to school or even liked that kind of learning.

Some Practical Applications for Educational Planning

I have intentionally used the terms *intellectual* and *cognitive capability* interchangeably. I would now define them, in terms of cognitive power, as the ability of individuals to form and pattern the world in which they live in such a manner as to construct the goals they will seek to achieve and to order their approach to the achievement of those goals. They will use their knowledge, experience, and skills in doing so and will seek goals in line with their interests. But the overall form and pattern of their construction, and the scale or extension of context of that construction, will represent the expression of their cognitive power.

Cognitive complexity is expressed in the number and range of variables that individuals use in constructing their worlds. This cognitive complexity is, I believe, the expression of cognitive power and is measurable in time frame.

But now let us examine some practical applications of this approach to intellectual development: a problem-solving approach to education, assessment and grouping of students, and the transition from school to work.

The use of problem-solving exercises or projects has a history of regularly coming into fashion and just as regularly going out of fashion again. It should have a solidly established place. One of the implications, however, of stratified system theory is that problem-solving projects should be tailored to the time frame of students. Students need to complete goals that require substantial periods of time to achieve and which put them on their true mettle.

The time scale would extend from five to ten minutes for younger children and less capable children on up to two or three months for some of the older and more capable children. The significance of such projects is that they allow pupils to experience their cognitive power to the fullest. And with such experiences, they will find their ability to cope with uncertainty being pulled out to full stretch. The art is to design appropriate projects to the time scales involved (Jaques, 1971).

The difficulty with such projects is that they do not readily fit in with standardized and "objective" grading. The substitute for such grading could, however, be that of a teacher's recording of the maximum time span over which students could be targeted to pursue and achieve given goals. The time spans thus identified would provide as useful a piece of information about a student's potential in work career as any amount of so-called objective examination results.

Problem-solving project work might be facilitated by putting students who are of roughly congruent time frames in the same class. Before describing such groups, however, I want to make one thing very clear. I am not arguing either in favor of comprehensive schooling or against it. But to the extent that some opportunity for grouping on the basis of cognitive power is deemed to be desirable, our work would point to the following principles.

On the assumption that it is possible to assess level of cognitive ability in time frame, in children as in adults, grouping in terms of cognitive mode would follow the pattern shown in Figure 6.10.

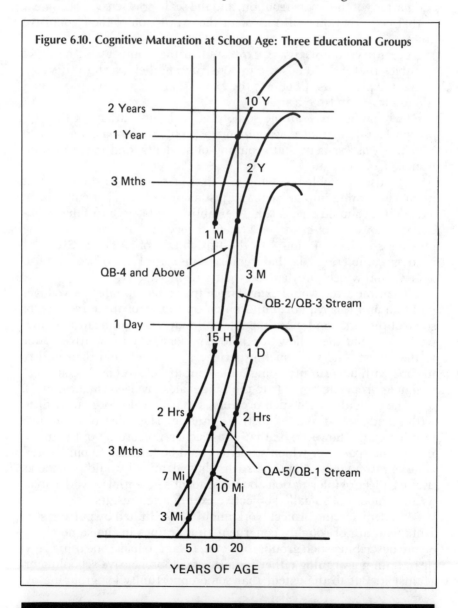

Figure 6.10. Cognitive Maturation at School Age: Three Educational Groups

The following groups have been separated out: children maturing in Mode I, in Modes II and III, and in Modes IV and higher. Roughly 45 percent of school children would fall into each of the first two groups, and the remaining 10 percent would fall into the third group.

The rationale for such a grouping is that Mode I group members work in the same way and, at any given age, in roughly the same time scale. They are most comfortable in concretely specified situations, with their penchant for physical doing. The Mode II and Mode III groups operate in longer time scales and require opportunity for expressing their capabilities for reflective formulation of what they are doing, as well as for formulating what might be, as illustrated above.

The third group should be composed of the students in Mode IV and above. The reason for keeping this group together is that they are all operating in a frame of reference in which they are comfortable handling generalizations. This ease with general categories is in contrast to the Mode II and Mode III groups who, while able to formulate what they are doing, nevertheless need to be solidly and concretely in direct physiological–perceptual contact with the object of their doing.

It might be that by, say, 15 years of age, students who are operating in maturation Modes VI and VII and who will eventually be capable of operating at strategic levels of work, should be given the opportunity to work together. There are, however, so few (less than 1 percent) that special classes might be impractical. But they should be recognized and identified and given special educational opportunities consistent with their extended time frames and capabilities.

There might, of course, be many reasons why children with the capability to work at these cognitive levels may not exercise that ability in work and study. Effective performance can be hindered or disrupted by emotional disturbance, lack of motivation, social alienation, family economic distress, or lack of support. But there is no sense, where grouping of children is being carried out, in compounding these difficulties by grouping children of high cognitive power (long time frames) but low achievement with students of equivalent achievement but significantly shorter time frames. To be required to work below one's time frame is frustrating, demotivating, and soul-destroying. It would be much better to keep students together with their equals in cognitive power and to remediate whatever shortcomings in psychological tools and orientation are impairing their achievement.

Finally, the transition from school to work should also be geared in accordance with these groupings. The longer the time frame of the student, the longer the student should continue with "purely academic" study. Vocationally oriented education might start at 14 to 16 years of age for Mode I students and could be extended up to 21 or 22 for the Mode II and Mode III students. The students at Mode IV and above should have their educations left as open as possible throughout undergraduate university education, with vocational tapering off after finishing the first degree level—in professional schools such as law, medicine, engineering, or perhaps by going straight into work without a vocational educational transition period.

There is substantial advantage to be gained by considering students in terms of their cognitive power as measured in time frame and cognitive mode, rather than in terms of IQ or examination grades. It gives students a chance to show their real work potential regardless of social, racial, or ethnic background, and regardless of sex. And it puts the proper emphasis on the ability to perform real work, as opposed to answering examination questions.

References

Bruner, J., and others. *Studies in Cognitive Growth.* New York: John Wiley, 1966.

Evans, John. *The Management of Human Capacity.* Bradford, England: MCB Books, 1979.

Gibson, R.O., and Isaac, D.J. "Truth Tables as a Formal Device in the Analysis of Human Action." In *Levels of Abstraction and Logic in Human Action.* Edited by E. Jaques, R.O. Gibson, and D.J. Isaac. Exeter, N.H., and London: Heinemann Educational Books Ltd., 1978.

Harvey, O.J.; Hunt, E.D.; and Schroder, H.M. *Conceptual Systems and Personality Organization.* New York, London: John Wiley, 1961.

Homa, Edna. "The Dynamic Interrelationships Among Work, Payment and Capacity." Doctoral dissertation, Harvard University, 1967.

Isaac, D.J., and O'Connor, B.M. "A Discontinuity Theory of Psychological Development." In *Levels of Abstraction in Logic and Human Action.* Exeter, N.H., and London: Heinemann Educational Books Ltd., 1978.

Jaques, Elliott. *Equitable Payment.* Exeter, N.H., and London: Heinemann Educational Books Ltd., 1961.

Jaques, Elliott. *Time-Span Handbook.* Exeter, N.H., and London: Heinemann Educational Books Ltd., 1964.

Jaques, Elliott. *Progression Handbook.* Exeter, N.H., and London: Heinemann Educational Books Ltd., 1968.

Jaques, Elliott. "Learning for Uncertainty." In *Work, Creativity and Social Justice.* Exeter, N.H., and London: Heinemann Educational Books Ltd., 1971.

Jaques, Elliott. *A General Theory of Bureaucracy.* Exeter, N.H., and London: Heinemann Educational Books Ltd., 1976.

Jaques, Elliott. *Free Enterprise, Fair Employment.* New York: Crane, Russak & Co; and London: Heinemann Educational Books Ltd., 1982a.

Jaques, Elliott. *The Form of Time.* New York: Crane, Russak & Co.; and London: Heinemann Educational Books Ltd., 1982b.

Jaques, E.; Gibson, R.O.; and Isaac, D.J., eds. *Levels of Abstraction in Logic and Human Action.* Exeter, N.H., and London: Heinemann Educational Books, Ltd., 1978.

Krimpas, G.E. *Labour Input and Theory of the Labour Market.* London: Duckworth, 1975.

MacDonald, Ian. "Five Levels of Mental Handicap." In *Levels of Abstraction in Logic and Human Action.* Edited by E. Jaques, R.O. Gibson, and D.J. Isaac. Exeter, N.H., and London: Heinemann Educational Books Ltd., 1978.

McNeil, Hector; Jaques, Elliott; and Nicoll, William. "Report of a Review of the Organization of the Commercial Relations and Export Promotion Work of the Board of Trade," 1969.

Richardson, Roy. *Fair Pay and Work.* Exeter, N.H., and London: Heinemann Educational Books Ltd., 1971.

Rowbottom, Ralph, and Billis, David. "Stratification of Work and Organisational Design." In *Levels of Abstraction in Logic and Human Action.* Edited by E. Jaques, R.O. Gibson, and D.J. Isaac. Exeter, N.H., and London: Heinemann Educational Books Ltd., 1978.

Stamp, Gillian. "Assessment of Individual Capacity." In *Levels of Abstraction in Logic and Human Action.* Edited by E. Jaques, D.J. Isaac. Exeter, N.H., and London: Heinemann Educational Books Ltd., 1978.

Stamp, Gillian. "Levels and Types of Managerial Capability." *J. Mgt. Studies* 18, 3 (1981).

Streuffert, S., and Streuffert, S.C. *Behavior in the Complex Environment.* New York: John Wiley, 1978.

7. Can Computers Improve the Thinking of Students in American Schools?

THE POWER OF THE COMPUTER IS WELL DOCUMENTED. WE HEAR ABOUT the amazing speed with which computers can handle vast quantities of information and solve millions of problems in a few seconds. And we're told that these machines have or will have the capacity to "think." This is real power.

Expectations result from knowing that power exists. When a new drug is tested and proved powerful, people soon start to use it in areas other than the one in which its power was established. When methods for resolving conflict prove effective or powerful in social situations, people immediately apply these methods in other areas, such as business settings. In both of these cases, the outcome of extending a powerful treatment to a new situation is not always positive.

The powerful computer, proven in so many applications, creates expectations (not hopes) that it will be powerful in all applications. Technocrats, for example, tell us that computers will be the salvation of learning in America.

In ten years [through the use of computers], we can turn around three generations of poverty in inner city schools.

This statement, which appeared in the *Washington Post* on June 16, 1965, was made by Bruce Merrifield, then Assistant Secretary of Commerce for Productivity, Technology, and Innovation. Unfortunately, history has not agreed with Merrifield. In fact, if we continue using computers as we have been, the impact on America's ability to write, read, add, and think will be negligible.

Connecting School Experiences

The concept of integration is mentioned often by those who write about thinking and about curriculum elements that will improve the quality of student thinking. This concept refers to the ability of creative thinkers to connect nonobvious aspects of experience. It is the ability to identify common elements in uncommon events that distinguishes the active mind from the routine mind. The "grand synthesis" is the direction, if not the goal, of the creative thinker.

In a similar manner, the goal of the most significant, if not the most popular, curriculum developers in the United States has been to provide students with an opportunity to find the connections among events often studied in isolation. In such landmark efforts as "Man A Course of Study," the social, political, economic and political aspects of life are concurrently examined because of their relatedness. In contrast, the teaching of organic chemistry as one chemistry and inorganic chemistry as another chemistry is a classical example of the artifical partitioning of theory and experience that has historically occurred in curriculum development.

Schools, therefore, have a mixed record of providing students with integrated curriculum experiences, regardless of our general acceptance that good education and good thinking emphasize the interrelated or integrative aspects of phenomena.

Nonintegrative Use of Computers in Schools

The applications of computer technology both reflect and exacerbate fragmentation of school curriculums. The lack of computer integration in the overall curriculum is evident in three ways computers are commonly used in any school where computers have been purchased in any reasonable quantity.

Computer Usage as a Reward

In many classrooms, where the entertainment value of computers is recognized, teachers use absorbing learning games as rewards for good classroom behavior. The educational software used in these situations is generally entertainment oriented rather than mastery oriented. In other words, the student plays, rather than works, with the computer. Progress is rarely measured so neither the child nor the teacher knows whether these entertainment sessions are helping or confusing the child in academic areas.

Even when software provides a face-valid concept and a powerful presentation, the content is most likely only peripherally connected to the curriculum of the classroom. Students are confronted with a series of discontinuous curriculum events, which only hampers teachers when they try to help students see the connections between school experiences where relationships are not planned.

Computer Usage as Literacy

A second nonintegrative use of computer appearing in the public schools is the "computer literacy" movement. The computer literacy strategy is one in which schools teach students how to program computers, thereby protecting them from some anticipated deprivation in later life.

It would be foolish not to have students understand the relationship of logic, physics, engineering and so forth that underpin the creation and operation of computers. It would be foolish not to discuss the ethical and moral consequences of having computer power, as we do the other powers we have (press, economic, military). But even at a practical level, the programming used and taught on microcomputers has little to do with the fourth and fifth generation languages that most professionals will be expected to use. Becoming familiar with current microcomputer programming languages is unlikely to help a student succeed professionally.

The outcome is that the schools have just shoved another vocational education program into an already crowded school day. What makes this a little different is its appeal to the middle and upper classes—much as egg painting might have been a hundred years ago. But the result is another example of nonintegrative additions to the overloaded school curriculum. This can only weaken teachers' attempts to connect this fragmented intellectual experience.

Computer Usage as a Secret Tutorial

A third nonintegrative aspect of the schools' use of computers is found in the computer's very private relationship to the person using it. The computer and the student enter into a "black box" arrangement. In the classroom, where the students are reading books, working in workbooks, performing experiments, or writing papers, education has a "public" aspect. A well-trained adult, and even one not so well trained, can usually figure out what students are doing and determine the kind of things to say to encourage students to understand the relationships between their work and more complex issues.

Unfortunately, most of today's instructionally oriented computer software does not reveal a great deal about what is going on to teachers or parents or anyone else who happens to be in the vicinity. The computer does not allow you to estimate progress with a glance as a workbook or lab experiment might allow. The computer gives the teacher little opportunity to diagnose student conceptual or social problems, as can be done in settings where students are engaged in more "public" learning. In some situations, the software does not even provide sufficient information about students' mastery of subjects covered in the programs. Computers and students become the black box in which the teacher is not allowed to look. Only the students know what they are doing. The teacher loses control and cannot help students integrate experience at the computer with the overall program of the classroom or school.

How Can Computers Be Successful in the Schools?

Three general areas seem highly probable for successful use of computers in schools.

Necessary Support for Drill and Practice

First, computers can provide the absolutely necessary drill and practice necessary for mastery of many important areas of the school's curriculum.

Yet drill and practice is often discounted by the academic community, even though it is the method we have used to master specific academic areas. It is especially critical for students who come from homes where conventional curriculum topics are not supported.

For some families, the school is a necessary source for remodeling, rehearsal, and practice. Children from such families rarely see or hear the basic rules of many subject areas utilized outside of school. They do not have the supervision, extra time, or support needed to practice the skills that stem from basic curriculum concepts.

Students need to practice. They need to practice what they have been taught so that they can use what they have been taught. Teachers simply do not have the time to give individualized drill and practice to each student in their classes, much less evaluate the results and provide feedback to students.

Necessary Support to the Distribution of Complex Curriculums

A second highly probable area for success is using computers to make complex curriculums universally available. Subjects like the basic skills can be taught well on computers because they have the advantage of being well defined, highly teachable through tutorial instruction, and politically attractive. However, you only need the first component, a well-defined topic, to create a successful computer application. There are other curriculum areas where broad scale access might depend on the use of a computer to provide the expertise necessary to "teach" in a difficult area. The computer will never play all roles or even the most significant roles in making access to complex curriculums available in all schools. However, the computer may allow curriculum developers to break the teaching, evaluating, prescribing tasks into more parts, thereby allowing training to focus on a few very achievable but critical tasks that only teachers can perform.

Necessary Support for Improving Overall Productivity

Every time a new idea comes along, it seems to take time from school days and energy from teachers. If the computer is going to be widely adopted in the schools, it must do the opposite. The power of the computer to improve efficiency has already been proven in the schools. However, the proof comes from applications in the administrative offices, not from applications in classrooms. As noted earlier, some things need to be learned through repeated rehearsal and practice. The schools are confronting a number of students who arrive at advanced levels of schooling without basic skills. What can you say about the productivity of the schools when the output is near zero? It is a very unproductive school whose students cannot spell, write functionally, or use reasonable grammar. There is no question that computers can reduce this low productivity without adding to the burdens of teachers. The computer can improve the management of the most important resources in students' intellectual development. These resources are the energies and aspirations of students, teachers, parents, and administrators. The computer may provide the modern, high pupil-teacher ratio school its only opportunity to coordinate these energies into a partnership.

Student/teacher productivity. Students have a certain amount of time available to learn under the supervision of the school. Because it is critical to utilize that time well, students need to confront the right task at the right level. The computer is a proven device for monitoring ongoing activity, for testing progress, and for branching to appropriate next steps.

Parent productivity. The number of studies showing the significance of parent involvement in the education of children continues to grow. Yet how many parents really have access to sufficient information to understand what their children are doing in school, much less play any role in supporting the school's curriculum?

Information is almost always general. If you ask what subjects a child is pursuing, you may get an answer as broadly staed as "reading" and "mathematics." If you ask for a diagnosis of strengths and weaknesses, you may get an answer as broadly stated as "has trouble with reading" or "needs help on number facts."

However, teachers cannot be asked to accept the administrative burden for reporting such information beyond what they are already attempting to do. This is a task ideally suited for a technical solution.

Software is now available to provide reports to both the teacher and the parent on how much progress the child is making and in what areas additional work is needed. Teachers with five or fewer students could provide such reports themselves. But teachers with well-designed computer software can do so for 20 or 40 students.

School administrator's productivity. Since most information about a child's performance is never recorded, the executive leadership in school buildings and district offices has little concrete information about curriculums presented in classrooms or the output of those efforts.

Principals who argue for more people, books, or computers rarely base their arguments on the impact of previous purchases. They simply don't have that information. To have information, something needs to be recorded at the source . . . in the classroom. To receive information, someone needs to organize the data and put them into an understandable format. Finally, to read information, someone has to make a written report. Teachers are always the logical source, but they are always overloaded.

This, then, is another opportunity for using existing software that provides executives reports for the school administrator without requiring additional people to record, organize, or report.

What Schools Need From the Next Generation of Software

One of the problems with the first generation of education software is that it has not gone far enough to assist schools' efforts to improve the intellectual status of students. Ironically, it has also made computers a burden—rather than a productive tool—to many teachers. There are five specific needs that schools will require of software in the remainder of this decade.

1. *Focus on current curriculum priorities:* the ability to focus on basic skills and curriculum areas regarded as high priority by the school community.

2. *Ensure mastery:* the ability to provide small modules with built-in evaluations that can be tailored to fit individual education programs.

3. *Keep the teacher informed and in control:* the ability to provide reports to teachers on student progress and remediation requirements.

4. *Inform parents:* the ability to generate reports that parents can use to support educational efforts.

5. *Support principals' resource decisions:* the ability to provide reports to principals on the overall progress of students and on the use and value of computers being used for instruction.

Questions Supporting Software Accountability Standards

How is this vision of a new generation of integrated educational computer software different from the programs used in most schools today? There are some questions which should be asked by all adults concerned about maximizing students' intellectual development before software purchases are made:

1. How do you know the concepts being taught by existing software are the ones children will be expected to know in order to succeed in school?

2. How does the software help students know (a) where to start, (b) what to do next, and (c) how things are going?

3. How does the software help teachers know (a) where all students are, (b) which students seem to be having the most trouble, and (c) whether time is being spent where effort is most needed?

4. How does the software help teachers with diagnostic and prescriptive testing?

(a) Is there detailed information about correct and incorrect responses from each student?

(b) Is there information about the learning style of students?

(c) Can reports be generated for parent-teaching meetings?

5. How does the software help principals with information about (a) which computers are being used, (b) what they are being used for, and (c) how fully computers are being used, in terms of time.

6. How does the software help with reports on (a) special students and special programs, and (b) student progress and products that can be shown to parents?

Quality software is software that connects with the ongoing curriculum. It is software that provides the necessary basic drill and practice, assists in the implementation of highly complex curriculums, and improves overall school productivity.

With quality software, the computer can and will improve the thinking of students in American schools. The problem is getting started.

About the Authors

Howard Gardner is Co-Director, Harvard Project Zero, Cambridge, Massachusetts.

Allan A. Glatthorn is Professor of Education, Graduate School of Education, University of Pennsylvania, Philadelphia.

Elliott Jaques is Professor of Sociology and Director, Institute of Organization and Social Studies, Brunel University, England.

Frances R. Link is Vice President, Curriculum Development Associates, Inc., Washington, D.C.

Garry L. McDaniels is President, Test Master, Inc., Washington, D.C.

A. Harry Passow is Jacob H. Schiff Professor of Education, Department of Curriculum and Teaching, Teachers College, Columbia University, New York City.

Robert J. Sternberg is Professor of Psychology, Yale University, New Haven, Connecticut.

Joseph M. Walters is Research Associate, Harvard Project Zero, Cambridge, Massachusetts.